ENDORSEMENTS

When I met Jesus face to face, He shared with me how when we truly love and value people and make them feel secure, that's when we make disciples for life. In his book, *Carrying the Presence*, Ryan shares with the reader how to do just that—making disciples of all nations. Through life experiences and revelation of the heart of God, Ryan will show you how to truly bring the Kingdom of God to anyone, anywhere!

DR. KEVIN ZADAI
Author of *Praying from the Heavenly Realms* and
The Agenda of Angels
www.kevinzadai.com

I see the heart of God in Ryan Bruss' new book, *Carrying the Presence*. The Word teaches us that the greatest demonstration of the supernatural love of God is that He sent Jesus to rescue us from sin and death. (John 3:16) In a fresh and practical way, Ryan teaches and inspires the reader to go out and rescue the world by manifesting the kingdom of God and making disciples for Jesus through the demonstration of both the supernatural love and power of God. Even seasoned soul winners and people in ministry will be refreshed and the fire for souls in them reignited, as they receive from the breath of the Spirit of God that is contained in the message of this book!

APOSTLE GUILLERMO MALDONADO
King Jesus International Ministry
Miami, FL

Ryan Bruss has made a case for loving people into Jesus that is both compelling and refining. He has created a fast track to the harvest by simply empowering our responsibility to love well. At the same time, he takes away all of our religious excuses for why we aren't reaching people—by reinforcing a love-based theology that makes up the nature of Jesus. Reading a book by someone with such different life experiences and training to my own, who shared his version of a beautiful compelling message, encouraged me. Read it, and you will be ignited into a full-fledged passion to love people the way Jesus did!

SHAWN BOLZ
www.bolzministries.com

Ryan Bruss reveals the very heart of God in his latest book, *Carrying the Presence*. As we prepare for the greatest revival this world has ever seen, the cry of the Spirit is, "Souls, souls, souls." Oh, what joy filled my heart as I read this book. Such a lightness in my spirit. Ryan says, "Everyone is called to share the good news of Jesus." This book will equip you to be a part of God's great end-time army. There is an anointing present that will awaken the heart of God in your life.

LIL DE FIN
Great-granddaughter of Smith Wigglesworth

In this book Ryan encapsulates the essence of the Gospel message. God loves and so should we. The world will know we are true followers of Jesus by our love for one another. In an age when so much divides us in the church, I pray this book will touch your heart in a greater way to pursue and remember the greatest of all IS love.

DR. RODNEY HOWARD-BROWNE
Revival Ministries International
Tampa, Florida

What an encouraging book! The testimonies and amazing quotes alone are worth the read, but the fact that they are beautifully linked with really practical and helpful teaching makes this a very fresh and inspiring tool for equipping everyone to reach out to others and make an eternal difference. Ryan's humility and transparency enables us all to easily relate to and be inspired by this wonderful teaching tool. I enjoyed this book from beginning to end as every chapter has wonderful testimonies of what can happen when we love people enough to step outside of fear and share the good news of the Gospel. The harvest is ripe and this book will equip you to fulfill the Father's desire to see people receive His invitation of salvation and relationship.

KATHERINE RUONALA
Author of *Living in the Miraculous, Wilderness to Wonders,* and *Life with the Holy Spirit*
Senior leader of Glory City Church Brisbane
and the Glory City Church Network
Founder and facilitator of the Australian Prophetic Council

Carrying the Presence will inspire you to step out in faith and demonstrate God's love and power to people wherever you go. Be encouraged by Ryan's prophetic encounters and moved by his powerful stories to share the authentic gospel of Jesus to those around you. I recommend leaders use this as a useful handbook for reaching out.

ALISS CRESSWELL
Author of The Normal Supernatural Christian Life
www.alisscresswell.com

The supernatural anointing of the Holy Spirit and the personal assistance He bestows on those who rely on God is the difference between boredom and excitement, duty and heartfelt devotion, and talking about versus living the abundant life the Bible teaches us we can experience. Any presentation of the gospel that reduces Christianity to a series of intellectual statements or ethical demands robs it of the power and joy God intended believers to possess. God has raised up a new generation of believers who are unwilling to settle for a powerless, boring Christian life and Ryan Bruss is one of them. In his book, *Carrying the Presence*, he shares with you his experience of the Kingdom of God that is unshaken, unstoppable, and triumphant. I heartily recommend this book to every believer.

JOAN HUNTER
Author/healing evangelist
www.joanhunter.org

Luke 17:21: *"Neither shall they say, Lo here! or, lo there! for, behold, the kingdom of God is within you."* I have known Ryan as a revivalist, passionate for Jesus, and a lover of souls. He burns with God's fire to reach the lost and manifest the Kingdom of Heaven to this generation. When we realize that all power resides inside of us, manifesting God's kingdom becomes a joy and a true satisfaction. May the Lord use this book and Ryan to awaken the consuming fire from God that will turn this world upside down!

RICH VERA
Prophet and revivalist
Founder of Voice of Healing Outreach
Orlando, Florida
www.richvera.com

I have had the blessing of getting to know Ryan and talking in depth with him about the Kingdom of God and his passion to see people brought to a realization of how much God loves them and what that means to them personally. I guarantee that when you read his new book *Carrying the Presence*, this same passion will come on you and you too will desire to be the hands and feet of Jesus everywhere you go. The Bible tells us in First John 4:17 that as Jesus is, so are we in this world, and this book will help teach you how that is possible right now, for you and every other believer!

BRUCE VAN NATTA
Author of *Saved by Angels* and *A Miraculous Life*
President and founder of Sweet Bread Ministries

Many books teach that God wants His children to share their faith. *Carrying the Presence* skillfully teaches people how! Every page is packed with practical wisdom easily understood by all. This book is destined to inspire you, your family, and those in your ministry to reach everyone, everywhere with God's undying love. More than just a how-to manual, Ryan Bruss tenderly releases the Father's heart and shepherds us to live lifestyles that make Jesus irresistible to the hardest of hearts. This book is a definite must-read for every church leader, disciple-maker, and child of God.

STEVE HANNETT
Founder, EveryHouse
TV Host, *The Miraculous Life*

CARRYING

the

PRESENCE

HOW TO BRING THE KINGDOM OF GOD
TO ANYONE, ANYWHERE

RYAN BRUSS

DESTINY IMAGE® PUBLISHERS, INC.

P.O. Box 310, Shippensburg, PA 17257-0310

"Promoting Inspired Lives."

This book and all other Destiny Image and Destiny Image Fiction books are available at Christian bookstores and distributors worldwide.

Cover design by Eileen Rockwell
Interior design by Terry Clifton

For more information on foreign distributors, call 717-532-3040.

Reach us on the Internet: www.destinyimage.com.

ISBN 13 TP: 978-0-7684-4863-4
ISBN 13 eBook: 978-0-7684-4864-1
ISBN 13 HC: 978-0-7684-4866-5
ISBN 13 LP: 978-0-7684-4865-8

For Worldwide Distribution, Printed in the U.S.A.

3 4 5 6 7 8 / 23 22 21 20 19

DEDICATION

I DEDICATE THIS BOOK TO JESUS AND HIS BEAUTIFUL WORDS that I carry close to my heart:

> *The harvest is great, but the workers are few. So pray to the Lord who is in charge of the harvest; ask him to send more workers into his fields. …Go and announce to them that the Kingdom of Heaven is near. Heal the sick, raise the dead, cure those with leprosy, and cast out demons. Give as freely as you have received!* (Matthew 9:37-38; 10:7-8 NLT)

ACKNOWLEDGMENTS

I WANT TO THANK ALL THE MEN AND WOMEN OF GOD WHO have poured into me throughout my life. There are too many to name them all one by one.

Special thanks to one of the greatest revivalists this world has ever known—my mentor, the beloved, late Steve Hill. Thank you to my father-in-law and friend, Dr. Michael Brown—a continual inspiration and example of a true man of God. Thank you to my beautiful wife Megan who has always encouraged me to seek God with all my heart and carry His heart to the world. Thank you to all those who call our Antioch House Church their home—love you all. Thank you, Sid Roth—a general in the faith and true soul-winner. Special thanks to Dr. Kevin Zadai whose ministry has taught me how to encounter the depths of God. Special thanks to Dr. Keith Ellis for his love and prophetic insight. A very special thank you to my mom for her love and continual intercession.

Finally, thank you to my friends Larry Sparks, Tina Pugh, Brad Herman, and everyone else at Destiny Image—without your help, this book would not be possible.

CONTENTS

FOREWORD
by Dr. Michael Brown

RYAN BRUSS IS ONE OF MY FAVORITE PEOPLE IN THE WORLD. He is full of life, full of the Spirit, full of the Word, full of Jesus. He is also my son-in-law. That means he is the husband of our younger daughter Megan and the father of our two eldest grandchildren, Elianna (now 18) and Andrew (now 15). How could I not love him? He has often been the life of our family gatherings and vacations. In fact, you will never have a dull family gathering if Ryan Bruss is there.

I remember driving through New York City with my wife, Nancy, and with Ryan and his family. We opened the window while he sang opera (or, what sounded like opera) at the top of his lungs, to the amusement of the folks on the streets. (Hey, this was New York, where almost anything goes.) That's Ryan!

But I'm not writing this foreword because Ryan is my son-in-law. I'm writing it because this book will change your life. Like Ryan, it is full of life, full of the Spirit, full of the Word, full of Jesus. I found myself praying as I read his words, freshly challenged to share my faith with others. The river of life within us wants to burst out and touch the world! Ryan helps show us the way—and I mean "us" as in each one of us, whether we're shy or bold, whether we're evangelists or home-schooling moms. The principles laid out in this book will work for anyone who loves Jesus.

Sometimes, due to my ministry schedule, I have to miss one of my classes at FIRE School of Ministry, and Ryan will fill in for me. Without fail, the Lord comes and touches the students when he is there. On one occasion, the Spirit began to fall on them the moment he walked through the door. On quite a few occasions, the class, which is supposed to go from 7:00 to 9:00 p.m., was still going at 10:00 or even 11:00 p.m. The students didn't want to leave. They were on their knees or on their faces, encountering God afresh.

Once, when returning after a trip, I asked the students how the class went with Ryan. One of the young ladies, about 20 years old and raised in the faith, said, "I never felt God like that in my life." Ryan really does carry the presence of the Lord, and in this book he will help you to do the same.

You say, "But I'm not like Ryan. Or like you, a professional minister. I have a hard time sharing my faith, and I really lack self-confidence."

Then this book is just what you need! First, the Scriptures that fill the pages will minister to you and build you up and challenge you and edify you. Second, the many examples Ryan shares from his own life will encourage you to take baby steps in being an outgoing witness. Third, the powerful quotes interspersed throughout the book will light a fresh fire within you. Fourth, the practical pointers that close out each chapter will guide you on your journey, literally step for step. It's amazing to see what happens when you put your toes in the water.

This book is also ideal for experienced soul-winners. You too will find fresh encouragement. Soon enough you'll find yourself swimming in deeper waters than ever, stepping out more in faith, not under carnal pressure but carried by the Spirit's love.

In fact, if there is one word that describes this book it is that word *love*. Love for Jesus. Love for your neighbor. Love for the hurting. Love for the lost. Love for the unlovable.

Ryan is here to tell you that that love is found in a person and His name is Jesus. That love we so desperately need is not something we can manufacture out of our own hearts and lives. It is not something we can work up or produce. It comes out of relationship with the Lord. It comes out of being in His presence. It comes out of saying, "God, in myself, I'm weak and selfish. But in You, I'm strong and full of love. Fill me afresh with your Spirit! I invite you to love this dying world through me." He will do it!

Some months back, when Ryan asked me if I would write the foreword to this book if I liked it, I told him absolutely—sight unseen. That's because I know him so well and trusted the content he would produce. Now that I have read it, I must say it exceeded my expectations. So much Scripture! So much life! So many powerful quotes! So many practical pointers!

I can't wait to hold the finished copy in my hands and tell my entire radio and TV audience to get a copy for themselves. And I can't wait for you to read the pages that follow. Not only will your own life be changed, but the lives of those around you will be changed as well.

Let's do this!

Dr. Michael L. Brown
Host, *The Line of Fire* radio broadcast
AskDrBrown.org

INTRODUCTION

by Heidi Baker

RYAN BRUSS AND I HAVE THE MOST IMPORTANT THING IN common—our first priority is to love God with all our heart, soul, mind, and spirit. This intimate relationship with the Living God motivates everything we do in life. All fruitfulness flows from intimacy. We also have the same second priority—to love people and communicate the Gospel to them. We want everyone we meet to see something hopeful and joyful in us and to feel Love pursuing them. That is exactly what this book, *Carrying the Presence*, is about. The Gospel is simple—love God and love people—but the Gospel message is one that is lived out daily, not just preached on a platform. We are all called to share this Good News and be the hands and feet of Jesus, meeting the needs of the "least of these," both the physically poor and those who are poor in spirit, downcast, depressed, and hopeless.

For some people, the desire to be used by God and share His love is there, but feelings of fear or insecurity, not knowing what to say or how to approach people, can be paralyzing. Ryan wrote this powerful book to activate the Body of Christ to share God's love every day. He tells his own personal stories, including many examples of people he shared God's love with, often in a very simple way. It is pretty incredible what God can do when you just start a conversation with someone! Ryan demystifies evangelism and explains, through these testimonies, how easy it is to share about Jesus. I believe as you read, your confidence and boldness will grow; you'll be reassured that God wants to use you too! You will become hungry to share the simple Gospel and see people's lives touched and changed.

I frequently talk about the message of "stopping for the one"—what I mean by that is asking God to show you at least one person to love each day. Thinking of it like that, as just one person who needs God's love, sharing the Gospel becomes easy and yet incredibly powerful. Imagine if you impacted one person's life each day with God's love? Imagine if every Christian did that? Stopping for the one can look like having an encouraging conversation with someone, buying a cup of coffee, washing dishes for your family member or housemate, or in my world in Mozambique, helping a child go to school and be blessed with food and water. It could be something big or something very small, but either way you are impacting someone's life. If you listen to Holy Spirit, He will show you the one in front of you who needs encouragement and love in Jesus.

One day, I was driving from Palm Beach, Florida, to Orlando. We stopped for a coffee and I sensed I should buy a journal at the convenience store in the rest stop. I didn't personally need a journal, and I didn't think it was for my friends with me, but I bought it anyway. Follow those little nudges! Then I saw a woman and her child. She looked like she was having a pretty rough day, and I immediately knew the journal was for her. As I gave it to her, I asked her how she was doing. I told her Jesus loves her and cares about her life. She began to cry and was very touched. All I did was buy a journal, say a few words, and pray for her. You can do that too! The more you listen and follow what you sense, the more of these experiences you will have. Ryan shares many stories like this where he followed Holy Spirit and people got deeply touched. He lives like this and his stories are powerful to read. Toward the beginning of the book, Ryan uses one of my favorite examples of stopping for the one, the story of The Good Samaritan.

In Mozambique, we perform this story as a drama on outreach. I love to get our children involved and create a skit that captures the audience's attention. I tell the story of a hurting man on the side of the road. Our kids pretend to beat him and steal his shoes and backpack—they are very good actors. Then, a blind worship leader walks by, a 24/7 worshiper on her way to the house of prayer...lost in song. Next, a blind preacher walks by on his way to a church growth conference. He wants to learn about how to build his church and reach people. They both walk by and do not stop for the one dying man lying on the road suffering. They don't see him, or at least they don't want to see him. They are not bad people; in fact, they are trying to follow God, but they are in a big rush to do something "important." At times we can become so focused on our own ministry agendas or growing in our Christian walk or being popular on social media that we miss the point completely. Jesus stopped for people. He didn't let ministry become so big that one person wasn't worth His time. The Samaritan was the most like Jesus in this story. He stopped, he had compassion, he shared his time, money, and resources. He loved well and that, Beloved, is the Gospel—that is the point.

Each and every day, could you make time to stop for at least one person? Jesus only did what He saw the Father doing, and He continuously stopped for people to love them and talk to them and heal them. He asked questions and genuinely cared about people—they weren't projects. The Bible said it was with compassion that He healed the sick. Can you let God move your heart with compassion too? Can you believe that you can have an impact? Can you trust that your smile, your tender words, your testimony backed by Holy Spirit can touch a hurting heart? It doesn't have to be complicated or difficult; it can be as simple as a smile.

All of us need to be reminded of this message sometimes. Whether you have been too scared to share your faith or whether you have shared so much that it has become a routine and not real connections, this book takes us back to the point of the Gospel—to save a lost and dying world through love. Read through this book and be encouraged again that you are the light of the world! You are the salt of the earth. Your life and words can bring healing and restoration or even just a smile in someone's day. We are all called to share the Gospel with both our words and our actions. This book is practical and encouraging, based both on Ryan living this out on a regular basis and on biblical examples. As you read, follow Ryan's applications and ask God to use you like never before. Get ready, He will do it!

—HEIDI G. BAKER, PhD
Cofounder and Chairman, Iris Global

Chapter 1

BEAUTIFUL PEOPLE

"Do you believe that God loves you beyond worthiness and
unworthiness, beyond fidelity and infidelity—that He
loves you in the morning sun and in the evening rain—that
He loves you when your intellect denies it, your emotions
refuse it, your whole being rejects it. Do you believe that
God loves without condition or reservation and loves you
this moment as you are and not as you should be?"
—BRENNAN MANNING,
All Is Grace: A Ragamuffin Memoir

THE WORLD CONSISTS OF BEAUTIFUL PEOPLE. I AM REFERRING
to the beauty that is found on the *inside* of every person whom
God has created. Even the worst of the worst of sinners is loved and created by God—*for God so loved the world* (see John 3:16). And everyone
who is breathing has the hope of becoming saved and spending an eternity with Jesus. No one *has* to go to hell. Hell is the choice of those who
reject what can only be found in Jesus.

The life of Paul the apostle comes to mind (see Acts 22). He certainly is an example of the depths that the Lord is willing to take to reach the seemingly unreachable.

Speaking of himself, Paul wrote:

> *Here is a trustworthy saying that deserves full acceptance:*
> *Christ Jesus came into the world to save sinners—of whom*
> *I am the worst* (1 Timothy 1:15 NIV).

Several years ago I had a vision where I found myself working in a factory alongside a conveyer belt. As the belt was moving, it was carrying along with it huge clogs of dirt about the size of basketballs. By the time these dirt clogs got to me, my job was to chisel away all of the dirt and rocks to get what was at the center. At the center of each clog was a very large, beautiful, sparkling diamond hidden within all of that dirt. The Lord spoke to me regarding this vision that part of my ministry would be to help people see their beauty and worth as He sees it. I'm telling you that Jesus defines beauty far, far different than our society does.

Almost any place you go in the world, you will find that most people judge beauty and worth by what they see on the outside. What people look like, how they talk, how they walk, how successful they are, etc. You find this thinking in the world and in the church. It's unfortunate that so many people place value and worth on what is standing before them or sitting next to them on the bus or working in the cubicle across from them or sitting next to them in school and on and on.

True beauty is defined by the way that God sees you—period. And how God sees and values us (saved and unsaved alike) is far different from how we see ourselves and others.

We so easily allow people, circumstances, pain, success, magazines, internet, etc. to define "who" we really are and "why" we are really here.

The result of this defining inevitably leads to personal frustration, low self-worth, hurt, anger, bitterness, pride, and the list goes on.

No matter who you are, to Jesus you are valuable. You are worth it. You are beautiful to Him. And when it comes to sharing Jesus and bringing the Kingdom of Heaven to the world around us, we must have the same heart toward others that Jesus has toward us.

My passionate desire is that through this book you will see the world around you completely different than you do right now. That you will begin to see how every single person is valuable, worth it, and has a calling, a destiny, and a purpose in God.

I have talked to hundreds of homeless people through the years and almost every single story that I have heard is not only captivating but heartbreaking. Many people abort their purpose in life because of sin and circumstances. Even as I write this, my heart is heavy and tears are flooding my eyes thinking about the people in this world who still need to be reached with the message of Jesus.

We have to remember that no prostitute ever dreamed of becoming a prostitute when they were playing with their dolls as a young child. No, she wanted to be a mom, a teacher, a wife, an astronaut, and so on. No drug addict ever dreamed of being a drug addict when they were running the bases and shooting hoops as a kid. They wanted to be the next NBA or MLB star. Yes, many people in this world have, by choice, made certain decisions that put them in prison, caused them to be homeless or prostitute themselves, or turn to a life of horrible greed as a CEO all the while rejecting God. However, Jesus came to seek and save the lost (see Luke 19:10). Jesus did not come to call the righteous but sinners to repentance (see Luke 5:32).

Remember that the only difference between you and someone (from gang members to millionaires) who is unsaved in this world is that you have met Jesus and they have not yet. Christians are no better than the rest of the world; we just found the answer to sin, sickness, and sadness and that is our wonderful Jesus. And we must introduce Him to CEOs, waitresses, flight attendants, prison inmates, family members, politicians, the hurting, the broken, and the dying. As a believer in Jesus, you happen to possess the answer within you—Jesus. These are the beautiful people Jesus is after.

Now, I will be the first one to say that not *everyone* is called to be an evangelist. I almost put that last statement as my very first line in this book because many Christians think that evangelizing is reserved for the evangelist and nothing could be farther from the truth. *Everyone* is called to share the Good News of Jesus. Everyone is called of God to bring the Kingdom of Heaven to others. Everyone. Here's a powerful quote by William Booth, the founder of the Salvation Army:

> "Not called!" did you say? "Not heard the call," I think you should say. Put your ear down to the Bible, and hear Him bid you go and pull sinners out of the fire of sin. Put your ear down to the burdened, agonized heart of humanity, and listen to its pitiful wail for help. Go stand by the gates of hell, and hear the damned entreat you to go to their father's house and bid their brothers and sisters, and servants and masters not to come there. And then look Christ in the face, whose mercy you have professed to obey, and tell him whether you will join heart and soul and body and circumstances in the march to publish his mercy to the world. —WILLIAM BOOTH

Now *that* is an intense quote, but one that we all need to hear. As a Christian, each one of us has a specific responsibility from God to our generation. Every one of us has the commission to "*go*" into all the world and preach the Gospel.

Did you ever realize that two-thirds of God's name is "go"? I know that may have made you chuckle, but the truth of the matter is that each one of us is called to go! However, "Go into all the world and preach the Gospel" means something different from one Christian to the next. Though you have a responsibility to bring to others the Kingdom of Heaven, how that responsibility is demonstrated is different for each one of us. Some are part of the five-fold ministry; some are artists, politicians, home group leaders, moms and dads, workers on college campuses, missionaries, coaches, police officers, and so on. But no matter what you are called do in this life, God wants you to bring the beautiful Gospel to the beautiful people He puts in front of you.

Let me give you an example of someone who has answered the call to "go." What I am about to say will liberate many people. We have someone who attends our house church named Janet whom I have known for over 20 years. She was saved and set on fire in 1995, during the Brownsville Revival. For many years after she was born again, she felt like she was supposed to be in vocational ministry because that just *seemed* like the right thing to do. Several well-meaning people had put pressure on her suggesting that if she was not in "full-time" ministry then she was not doing what God had called her to do. That's when she put tremendous pressure on herself to fulfill all of these expectations she was apparently supposed to live up to. After many years of "trying" to do the right thing and be the right person who is supposed to be in "full time" ministry, she let all of that go and just gave her future to God. She then decided to go to nursing school and it was one of the best decisions she has ever made. Not only is Janet thoroughly enjoying what she knows God called her to do, the stories that she shares of how she is bringing the Kingdom to those she comes in contact with through nursing are some of the greatest stories you will ever hear! She doesn't always get to share the Gospel, but she always shares love and many lives have already been impacted in the short time that Janet has been a nurse. Janet let go of what others wanted her to do and embraced what God has called her to do. I pray that more and more people will be like Janet and bring the Kingdom of Heaven to their places of influence.

I want you to take a moment and pray right now that God will begin to lead you to those to whom He wants you to bring the Kingdom of Heaven. Pray for love and compassion for those who will cross your path today.

The other day I was with my son at a sports store and the lady at the counter seemed to be wincing in pain so I asked her if she was okay. She said that her stomach really hurt. I grabbed her hand and asked her if she was a Christian and she said yes and we prayed for the healing power of God to come over her body. You see how easy that was? The Holy Spirit knew I was going in to that store and I could have walked up to any cashier, but God wanted to touch this precious woman. Incidentally, my son said to me on the way out that he loves to see me do that!

> He is not seeking a powerful people to represent Him. Rather, He looks for all those who are weak, foolish, despised, and written off: and He inhabits them with His own strength. —GRAHAM COOKE

You see, God wants to use each one of you to tell of His goodness, mercy, forgiveness, and love, and to show His power to those around you—those He puts in your path each day. It is much easier than you think to talk to people about Jesus and to bring the Kingdom to others. We will cover that more in a later chapter.

My personality is that I am very interested in people. I want to know their story. I want to know who they are and what they feel. We need to learn to take a genuine interest in people if we are going to bring the Kingdom to them. In this 21st century, it seems as if humanity has become so selfish and self-absorbed, so we all need to make sure we do not find ourselves in that category. There are people right now who are in your life or who you will meet shortly who need to hear that Jesus loves them and that He has a plan for their life. Will you tell them?

Ask the Lord to give you fresh eyes to see, ears to hear, and a heart to discern the beautiful people God has for you to bring the Kingdom to. Countless times I have asked the Lord to show me what He sees in certain people so I can have a heart of love and compassion for them. Like the vision I had, ask the Lord to show you those hidden, beautiful diamonds in people.

> Beauty is mysterious as well as terrible. God and the devil are fighting there, and the battlefield is the heart of man.
> —FYODOR DOSTOEVSKY

Now that you have an understanding of these "beautiful people," ask God to give you a heart for the world around you. Pray that you will see those you meet each day with the eyes of the Father. Guard your heart against being cold or apathetic toward people as *every* person you meet today is overwhelmingly loved by God.

Today, think of someone in your life (could be at work, at church, or even in your own family) who rubs you the wrong way. You may not even be able to put your finger on why they bother you—they just do! Now, as this person comes to mind, ask the Holy Spirit to reveal to you something wonderful and beautiful that He sees within that person. Once you have a word(s) or picture in your heart, pray into what you see and watch how your heart will change toward that person.

You have a calling on your life. This calling is to bring the Kingdom of Heaven to certain people in this world whom nobody else can. You are that unique and special to Heaven! Here's the good news—you can start today. Let go of the past and all of its baggage and embrace what God has for you today. Step into your destiny and watch how His plan unfolds before you. Your God adventure is awaiting you. It's time to get excited again!

Chapter 2

WHO REALLY IS MY NEIGHBOR?

"But God's love is big enough to touch any life, to make light out of any darkness. Jesus came that we might have life, so that no more would we have to die in depression, anger or pain. He loved people back to life. He would go anywhere, talk to anyone. And wherever He went, He would stop for the one—the forgotten one, the one who was rejected, outcast, sick, even stone dead. Even a thief who was dying for his crimes on the cross next to Him. In the Kingdom of God's love there is no sinner who cannot come home."

—HEIDI BAKER, *Learning to Love: Passion, Compassion and the Essence of the Gospel*

WHO IS MY NEIGHBOR? AND WHERE DO I FIND THESE BEAU-tiful people? I believe that Jesus brilliantly answered the "who is my neighbor" question in Luke 10:25-37:

And behold, a certain lawyer stood up and tested Him, saying, "Teacher, what shall I do to inherit eternal life?"

He said to him, "What is written in the law? What is your reading of it?"

So he answered and said, "'You shall love the Lord your God with all your heart, with all your soul, with all your strength, and with all your mind,' and 'your neighbor as yourself.'"

And He said to him, "You have answered rightly; do this and you will live."

But he, wanting to justify himself, said to Jesus, "And who is my neighbor?"

Then Jesus answered and said: "A certain man went down from Jerusalem to Jericho, and fell among thieves, who stripped him of his clothing, wounded him, and departed, leaving him half dead. Now by chance a certain priest came down that road. And when he saw him, he passed by on the other side. Likewise a Levite, when he arrived at the place, came and looked, and passed by on the other side. But a certain Samaritan, as he journeyed, came where he was. And when he saw him, he had compassion. So he went to him and bandaged his wounds, pouring on oil and wine; and he set him on his own animal, brought him to an inn, and took care of him. On the next day, when he departed, he took out two denarii, gave them to the innkeeper, and said to him, 'Take care of him; and whatever more you spend, when I come again, I will repay you.' So which of these three do you think was neighbor to him who fell among the thieves?"

And he said, "He who showed mercy on him."

Then Jesus said to him, "Go and do likewise."

The *certain* lawyer in this story was some sort of teacher or expert in the law and he stood up to test Jesus. He asked the most important question a man or woman could ever ask in this life—what shall I do to inherit eternal life?

Jesus totally set this teacher up by answering his question with a question. Always remember that when Jesus is asking you a question, He's not looking for information. Think about that for a moment.

This expert in the law went on to quote Deuteronomy 6:5 and Leviticus 19:18, the two greatest commandments in the Word of God: "'You shall love the Lord your God with all your heart, with all your soul, with all your strength, and with all your mind,' and 'your neighbor as yourself'" (Luke 10:27).

Everything in life and ministry flows from these two verses. Everything. And notice how both of these commandments are united by one main theme—*love*. We must learn as never before in this hour to keep the first commandment first place. This greatest commandment should be our heart's passion morning, noon, night, and midnight snack!

And when we fall in love with Jesus, I mean really fall in love with Jesus, it turns our whole life upside down and inside out. So friends, if you do anything in life well, do this well—love Him with everything. A heart that is abundantly satisfied in Him and that enjoys the pleasures of knowing and loving God—that person will never be shaken.

Now, loving our neighbor is *not* the greatest commandment, but it is second. And second on the Father's list is very, very important.

He who does not love does not know God, for God is love (1 John 4:8).

Why are we to love our neighbor? We are to love our neighbor because we love what Jesus loves. And He loves the rich, the poor, the dirty, the broken, those who have fallen into sin, the successful, the homeless, those on death row, those who have been battered by life—everyone.

You see, we hold the ability to love our neighbor. We have the power and ability through Jesus to choose to love. I was once talking to the Lord about someone I found difficult to love. I asked Jesus, "How should I love _____?" He replied quickly and tenderly, "As I have loved you." Enough said.

If we do the first commandment well, it will automatically spill over into the second commandment. For when we love Him with all of our heart, He pours out His love back to us. This radically changes us from the inside out and therefore it gives us a love for others and ourselves.

"Your neighbor as yourself." Did you catch that? I love *me* because He loves *me*. Even with all of my weaknesses and shortcomings. The stronger this identity is solidified within me, the greater the ability for me to love my neighbor.

> *As the Father loved Me, I also have loved you; abide in My love. ...This is My commandment, that you love one another as I have loved you* (John 15:9,12).

Our self-worth is not to be defined by our mistakes, how we were raised or by the opinions of others. Jesus settled the issue of our worth by walking the terrible and joyful journey to the cross for you and me. Our worth is defined by His everlasting and overwhelming love for us—every moment of every day. When we keep ourselves in the love of God, it gives us the right perspective on how He feels about us and others. Abide continually in His love, dear ones.

Try as you might, you will not authentically love your neighbor more than you feel loved by God. So many people struggle with loving others because they struggle with loving themselves.

We love God well when we learn to love what He loves—our neighbor. You see, love *makes* you my neighbor. Don't think of it this way: "You are my neighbor and therefore Jesus says I have to love you." No. Rather, "I love you, therefore *you are my neighbor.*" We have not lived well if we have not loved well.

When God called us to love our neighbors as ourselves, you know, He meant that. Think of the man who was beat up in our story. The Samaritan loved and cared for him the same way he would have wanted to be loved and cared for.

However, the expert in law wanted to justify himself and asked Jesus, "Who is my neighbor?" He was like, "Jesus, define neighbor for me. What do You *really* mean by that—neighbor?" He was looking for a way out by asking who his neighbor was.

Who do you think your neighbor is? This parable does not tell us in form who our neighbor is, but this parable does show us how true love is supposed to work in the Kingdom.

When it comes to those who we are to love, I realize that some people are more difficult to love than others. Especially those who have wronged us. People can be so ungrateful, rude, selfish, prideful, bitter, angry, and ungodly. And then there are those who don't even believe in God (I hope you caught that).

> *Then Jesus answered and said: "A certain man went down from Jerusalem to Jericho, and fell among thieves, who stripped him of his clothing, wounded him, and departed, leaving him half dead."*

This just sounds like the enemy who comes to steal, kill, and destroy (see John 10:10).

Many people you meet each day feel "half dead" on the inside. They may have lost their home, their job, fallen into sin, become brokenhearted; they may be hurting, suicidal, grieving, or hopeless. And they walk around day after day feeling "half dead" within their hearts.

Your neighbor can be your literal neighbor and it can also be those in church, at work, strangers you meet, and even those in your own home. As a pastor I have seen people who want to change the world and at home their spouse is "half dead" emotionally. Friend, this cannot happen. There are many people in church today who are a success at work, a success at church, and even a success at recreational activities. They seem to help everyone around them, but at home their wife is "lying on the side of the road half dead" emotionally and you have passed her by like the religious priest and Levite. You cannot be a "neighbor" to everyone else and neglect your wife and children. This is hypocrisy.

Listen, this man lying on the side of the road *may* have been doing something that he was not supposed to be doing. He may have been a thief himself. He may have been looking for a prostitute. Does that disqualify him from your love? Does that disqualify him from being your neighbor? Certainly not! Love is not selective.

> *Now by chance a certain priest came down that road. And when he saw him, he passed by on the other side.*

The priest and the Levite in this story knew the law but when it came time to live it out, they failed miserably. They didn't know the law of love. We see throughout the Gospels how the priests, the scribes, the Pharisees, the teachers of the law, the religious—they didn't get it. They did not live out the two greatest commandments that they were supposed to know so well—the commandments that clearly say that love must come first.

The special duty of the priest was to offer sacrifices at the temple—to present incense, to conduct the morning and evening services of the temple. But he passed by on the other side, maybe unconsciously trying to get as far away from the responsibility of love that he could. The priest did not even have the heart to at least check on him. And again, he was a priest. It's amazing how many excuses we come up with when the greatest thing we can do at the moment is love. The priest was too busy with religion and himself.

> *Likewise a Levite, when he arrived at the place, came and looked, and passed by on the other side.*

The Levites' duties were to assist the priests in their services. They took care of the temple, keeping it clean, and preparing supplies for the sanctuary such as the oil, and incense. This Levite looked more intently at the man than the priest, but also did not have enough love for him to do anything about his misery. Love is not selfish.

> *But a certain Samaritan, as he journeyed, came where he was. And when he saw him, he had compassion.*

There was real hostility between the Jews and Samaritans. The Samaritans were looked down upon. They had no dealings with each other. It doesn't say that the man lying there was a Jew. Maybe he was? Jesus does not tell us because it does not matter!

Through the years, people have labeled this story as "The Good Samaritan." But this Samaritan was good *before* this event happened. He did not have or need a supernatural anointing or a word from God to help this person. Love compelled him. This man lying there was his neighbor because he loved people.

Again, maybe this man lying there was up to no good. Maybe he owed the thieves money. Maybe he was also a thief. Maybe he was a nasty, hateful person who was full of pride. Maybe he was in the wrong place at the wrong time. Whatever the case may be, the Samaritan didn't first try to determine if he was worth helping. He simply had love and compassion. And a moment of kindness and compassion can be worth a lifetime of hope for a hurting heart.

> *So he went to him and bandaged his wounds, pouring on oil and wine; and he set him on his own animal, brought him to an inn, and took care of him.*

I absolutely love that verse. What love! He *poured* in the oil and the wine, freely giving it. It sounds like what we read in Isaiah 61:1-3:

> *The Spirit of the Lord is upon Me, because the Lord has anointed Me to preach good tidings to the poor; He has send Me to heal the brokenhearted, to proclaim liberty to the captives, and the opening of the prison to those who are bound; to proclaim the acceptable year of the Lord, and the day of vengeance of our God; to comfort all who mourn, to console those who mourn in Zion, to give them beauty for ashes, the oil of joy for mourning, the garment of praise for the spirit of heaviness; that they may be called trees of righteousness, the planting of the Lord, that He may be glorified.*

The oil and wine that the Samaritan man had were his for his own enjoyment and refreshment. Oil and wine were often used in medicine to heal wounds. You also have oil and wine for your neighbors in abundance as you spend time with Jesus.

Jesus doesn't merely say that the Samaritan showed kindness to the broken man, but He details the compassionate, caring heart that he had for him.

The wine represents the blood, forgiveness, cleansing, and healing. No matter what you've done. Again this could be someone in your own household, in your church, at work, or next door. The oil represents the refreshing, fragrant, comforting heart of the Holy Spirit. Doesn't that sound so wonderful?

We must live in abundance ourselves to be able to give it out to the world around us—our neighbors. If you barely have enough oil and wine for yourself (from lack of the first commandment), how are you going to do the second commandment well? Don't just pour out the oil and wine to others and not keep yourself filled up. Have oil and wine in abundance and it will simply overflow to your neighbors. You will meet people on a regular basis who God is wanting to pour in the oil and the wine, and you will find great joy in doing this as it's done from the heart of God.

The Samaritan put the man on his own animal and brought him to the inn. He was going all the way with this! I believe that the inn here can represent the Church. And not just any old traditional, religious church, but a church that has the same heart as the Samaritan. When a church is living in its destiny, it's ministering to the broken, wounded, and dying of the world and not passing them by on the other side of the road.

> On the next day, when he departed, he took out two dena-
> rii, gave them to the innkeeper, and said to him, "Take
> care of him; and whatever more you spend, when I come
> again, I will repay you."

The Samaritan spent the night with the wounded man, caring for him. This is a forgotten principle in our churches today. The privileged act of praying and pressing through for and with someone. So you lose a little sleep on a particular night, but you contended for your spouse in prayer. Or your kids, your boss, your unsaved loved ones. Love must be demonstrated not just in words but in actions. The Samaritan even gave of his money. When it comes to loving our neighbors, you may have to help financially. What's wrong with that? Remember, it's not about deserving, it's about love. And in Heaven, there is much reward for love.

> *Give, and it will be given to you: good measure, pressed down, shaken together, and running over will be put into your bosom. For with the same measure that you use, it will be measured back to you* (Luke 6:38).

Loving your neighbor may cost you time, money, and energy. Some people are easier to pour in the oil and wine and some are more difficult. Some wounds heal easily and some take a long time. This will show the extent of our love. Remember that Jesus never gave up on us (while we were yet sinners, see Romans 5:8). He freely paid the full price for us.

> *"So which of these three do you think was neighbor to him who fell among the thieves?" And he said, "He who showed mercy on him." Then Jesus said to him, "Go and do likewise."*

I think this teacher of the law was starting to get it.

Who is your neighbor? Wherever there is love, you will find your neighbor.

> The surest way to determine whether one possesses the love of God is to see whether he or she loves his or her neighbor. These two loves are never separated. Rest assured, the more you progress in love of neighbor the more your love of God will increase. —TERESA OF AVILA

One of the greatest passions of my life is to teach people how to live daily in the Father's love and embrace. It's learning to keep the first and greatest commandment first place in our lives. Today, ask the Father to remove everything in your life that is hindering wholehearted love. Ask Him to help you live out the first commandment like never before. Ask Him to fill you with His amazing love and then—just receive it! I pray that His love captivates every area of your life today. When you do this, you will have "oil and wine" overflowing in your life for you and for others.

In this chapter, you learned who your neighbor really is. Again, it could be your literal neighbor or someone at work, church, or even within your own home. Ask the Holy Spirit if there is someone today you can pour in a little "oil and wine" to minister to their hurting heart. It could mean that you simply tell someone that they are loved. It may be that today, the Holy Spirit is highlighting someone for you to buy a cup of coffee or a meal just to hear their heart so they feel loved. Remember, this is not about bringing the Kingdom to people who may "deserve" it or not, but about learning to love your neighbor.

Chapter 3

MY JOURNEY

*"But God doesn't call us to be comfortable. He calls us to trust Him
so completely that we are unafraid to put ourselves in situations
where we will be in trouble if He doesn't come through."*
—FRANCIS CHAN

I T WAS OVER 25 YEARS AGO WHEN I BECAME A YOUTH PASTOR IN Minnesota. Our little church was located in downtown Minneapolis very close to the "wild" areas of the city. And my young heart was burdened for the people I saw there. At that time I had very little experience sharing Jesus with total strangers. But this much I knew—Jesus loved me and He turned my life around, set my heart on fire, and I just had to tell others that they could experience the same. The apostle Paul was thinking along similar lines as we read in Philippians 3:12-14:

> *Not that I have already attained, or am already perfected;
> but I press on, that I may lay hold of that for which Christ
> Jesus has also laid hold of me. Brethren, I do not count*

myself to have apprehended; but one thing I do, forget-
ting those things which are behind and reaching forward
to those things which are ahead, I press toward the goal for
the prize of the upward call of God in Christ Jesus.

Essentially Paul was saying that he is going to get ahold of God the same way that God got ahold of him! And whatever that meant on this earth, Paul was willing to do that for God. Jesus ran after Paul and, in turn, Paul ran after Jesus. And this is what happened to me. I was just so thankful that the Father loved me and had a purpose for my life that I just wanted to do whatever I could to bring Jesus to a hurting, dying, and lonely world. And if the people who walked the streets of Minneapolis were not going to come to our church, then I was going to go to them. And basically that's where my journey started when it comes to bringing the Kingdom of Heaven to others.

It was during this time that you could find me and others from our church on a Friday night walking the streets of Minneapolis late into the night. Of course, I had a myriad of emotions flowing through me as I was watching all the people passing by. Who do I talk to? What do I say? What if they reject me or even hurt me? I was anxious, fearful, and felt out of place. But I knew that I knew that "He who is in you is greater than he who is in the world" (1 John 4:4).

So I know if I can do this, you can. The same Jesus who lives within me lives within you. The same Holy Spirit who flows through me flows through you. All you have to do is be willing. All you have to do is have a "yes" within your heart and God can use you. I promise.

During my time ministering on the streets of Minneapolis, I met people from all walks of life. Again, we would go late at night when most people were enjoying what people do when it gets dark. You know what I mean. I remember talking to three girls once who were smoking marijuana and blowing it back in my face as I shared the Gospel with them. They each grabbed one of the tracts from my hand and mockingly read John 3:16 in unison. I couldn't help but grieve for them, knowing that this scene would inevitably be replayed for them at the judgment seat if they did not turn to Christ.

We saw many people receive Jesus into their hearts during my time there but I must tell you that many also rejected Him.

> *Enter through the narrow gate. For wide is the gate and broad is the road that leads to destruction, and many enter through it* (Matthew 7:13 NIV).

You see, our job is to bring the Kingdom to others with love, faith, and the power of God. If they reject the message, they are not rejecting you but the One who sent you. However, I am a strong believer in planting spiritual seeds in the soil of people's hearts. They may laugh or mock me at the time, but that seed was planted, and they will never forget it. I really believe that. Because the Gospel is life, love, and power, it does not return void. Though they may still choose hell, the seed was planted in them.

> *So shall My Word be that goes forth from My mouth; it shall not return to Me void, but it shall accomplish what I please, and it shall prosper in the thing for which I sent it* (Isaiah 55:11).

After I began to stop and talk to people about Jesus during my first time, I literally felt the glory of the Lord completely surrounding me as I walked the streets. The glory of the Lord was so strong on me at times that I would find myself in the most incredible of circumstances. For instance, on a regular basis I would stop large groups of college students who were walking on the streets by standing in front of them (sometimes ten-plus people) and yelling, *stop!* Of course, they didn't know what was going on, but once I had their attention, I began to share

Jesus with them. I loved it. They laughed. But I knew Jesus loved it. Inevitably one or two in those big groups would stay behind to hear more. It was awesome.

Every Friday night there were hundreds of homosexuals on the streets because of a few very large bars that catered to their lifestyle. Some of the most interesting and intense conversations were with homosexuals. They are so broken, wounded, and bound up in their sin. I would see many things happening on the streets that I could not put in this book. But it was heartbreaking what I saw. I saw many older men dressed with wigs and full makeup going into the bars. I would stop as many of them as I could to share Jesus with them and offer to pray for them. They were some of the hardest people to reach with the Gospel because of their perverse lifestyle. Those demons did not want to let go easily. But God was faithful and many lives were touched.

I remember one time I was passing out Gospel tracts to every person who was entering in that particular bar. I must have passed out 50 to 75 tracts before the manager came out of the bar and placed a garbage can outside the door. As I was handing out the tracts, the manager encouraged those walking into the bar to throw it away. I looked at that manager and said, "If anybody was going to get born again after reading one of those tracts that you had them throw away, their blood is going to be on your hands." He got so scared that he grabbed the garbage can and ran inside! So I kept out passing the tracts. I was stationed in such a way that the people going in just assumed it was an advertisement. I can only imagine the conversations that were taking place in that bar, which could hold up to 3,000 people.

I never held a sign that said they were damned to hell because of their lifestyle. I never pointed my finger in their face and yelled at them. But I did minister to hundreds of homosexuals and lesbians with the power and love of Jesus. People who minister on the streets sometimes seem to yell loud at the people passing by to make up for a lack of love and power. Not all, but some. Truthfully, I am for any means of sharing the Gospel, as long as it is done in love. I have preached with a loud-speaker on the streets many times. I even had someone come and spit in my face as I shared about the love of God. I will share more about this later, but demons seem to be at their worst and manifest most aggressively when confronted on their dark territory with the power and blood of Jesus.

One particular evening while sharing Jesus with people, I saw hundreds and hundreds of people pouring out of a theatre about a block and a half away from the area that we usually ministered. I brought the team to that particular location and every single man had a tuxedo on and every woman was dressed in their finest. As we proceeded to share Jesus with these apparently "well-to-do" people, not one single person would have anything to do with what we were sharing—not one. Everyone either ignored us with disdain or laughed with sheer arrogance. I still remember this moment like it was yesterday. They were so hard-hearted and in another world. So I told the team to go back to the other block. When we got back to our regular location, it seemed like every single person wanted to hear what we had to say. Oh friend, how hard it is for the rich to enter the Kingdom of Heaven.

> *Then Jesus said to his disciples, "Truly I tell you, it is hard for someone who is rich to enter the kingdom of heaven. Again I tell you, it is easier for a camel to go through the eye of a needle than for someone who is rich to enter the kingdom of God." When the disciples heard this, they were greatly astonished and asked, "Who then can be saved?" Jesus looked at them and said, "With man this is impossible, but with God all things are possible"* (Matthew 19:23-26 NIV).

I will never forget those few years in Minneapolis. It was eye-opening and very fruitful. So many stories. So many broken people. I'm glad I was there for that season.

From Minnesota I moved to my hometown in Zion, Illinois where I worked for a construction company for a number of years. What a mission field! You see, God will use you wherever you are planted. He wants to use you right now at the job where He has placed you. You are not there by accident! Look around tomorrow at all the people you work with. They are no different from all those people I met on the streets of Minneapolis. They also desperately need Jesus.

So here I was building houses and praying for these men I worked closely with every day. When they were in one part of the house listening to Led Zeppelin or AC/DC, I was at the other end praising and worshiping Jesus. As Paul said in First Corinthians 5:10, we would literally have to be taken out of the world to avoid the world. As Christians, God has called us to live among unbelievers but to not do what they do or say what they say when it comes to sin. We are to come out from among them and be separate (see 2 Cor. 6:17). But I loved these guys and wanted to see them become born again. So I started a Bible study an hour before work twice a week, and most of them showed up! Some to make fun (in a lighthearted way), but most of them were interested, especially when one of the owners of the company would come. I remember so clearly one particular day as I was going through the book of John that I led many of them in a prayer to receive Jesus. That was a good day!

You see, I was not concerned what they thought of me. I just worked hard and tried to live my Christianity out loud. I wanted to bring the Kingdom of Heaven to a construction company. Did I make mistakes? Yes. Did I always represent Jesus the way that I wanted? No. But they watched the fruit of my life for several years and that's why I had their attention. They knew that this guy was for real. Being genuine and loving people will open many doors for you to express the Kingdom of Heaven.

From Zion, I moved to Pensacola, Florida in 1996 to be part of the great Brownsville Revival and the school of ministry there. It was during my time at the school that I got the burden again to minister on the streets. With that powerful revival taking place in Pensacola, the city was buzzing with much supernatural activity. I eventually started working for the school of ministry and we would take a few hundred—yes a few hundred—students out on the streets every Friday and Saturday night. And you can imagine how many stories of changed lives we saw over the years. Students would literally overwhelm certain parts of the city on a Friday night. And many, many unsaved people we met ended up getting down on their knees with us, and by the time they stood up they were a new creation (see 1 Cor. 5:17).

We saw many, many salvations and miracles. We would meet people who were literally on their way to commit suicide and instead they received Jesus. We led people to the Lord who were caught up in witchcraft, the occult, and satanism. We had a very large outreach to the Navy base in Pensacola, and many of those young sailors gave their lives to Jesus before they were shipped off. We had many students who would go to nursing homes and lead the elderly to the Lord. These precious souls would cry as we brought the Kingdom to them. Some even died soon after receiving the Lord. We were everywhere and we loved it. We even went to a few medium/maximum security prisons in Florida and Alabama on a regular basis, sharing our testimonies, leading many to Jesus.

With this many students sharing Jesus in so many places on a regular basis, we were not without problems. We were constantly threatened, spit at, verbally abused, people trying to run us over in cars, physically assaulted and so on.

But let me tell you of one of the greatest testimonies of a changed life that we saw on the streets of Pensacola. As I remember the story, a man by the name of Chacho was heading into a local bar with some of his friends. They were all met by a group of students who had been standing outside the bar sharing the Gospel. Chacho's friends went into the bar, but he was intrigued and stayed talking with the group of students. Chacho admitted to living a very worldly lifestyle and he wanted to change. He ended up getting on his knees with the students and repented for the way he was living and received Jesus into his heart. As he stood up, he was instantly set free from all the addictions in his life! Jesus gloriously changed him in a single moment. All because someone was bold enough to talk to him as he went into a bar. But that's not the end of the story. Chacho was discipled by a few students and became on fire for God. He was so thankful for all that God did for him that he wanted to serve God for the rest of his life. That was 20 years ago. As of today, Chacho and his close friend Marc have planted churches, orphanages, and feeding programs throughout Mexico! They have raised up many pastors and missionaries to extend the work of the Lord. They have yearly conferences, which I have had the privilege of preaching at a few times. Just last year I preached for him at an Israel conference that had about 1,000 people. Chacho is just as on fire and in love with Jesus as he has ever been. When I am with Chacho and Marc, I feel such a strong love for God and people coming from them. They are such an example of what a follower of Jesus should be like.

I shared this beautiful testimony with you as an example of just one life that was changed because of people simply bringing the Kingdom of Heaven to the world around them. You never know what God is doing in a heart as you talk with someone. Chacho was ready to receive Jesus. His friends were not. In fact, they tried to convince him to come back into the bar while the students were sharing with him. I want to cry just thinking about what may have happened to Chacho if those students weren't out there. It was truly a divine appointment.

I believe that it is God's intention to use His angels on a regular basis to set up divine appointments for us if we are willing to be used by God. We just have to open our hearts to what He is saying and doing around us. It's not a pressured thing. It comes natural. God uses ordinary days and ordinary moments and ordinary people to reveal Himself to the world around us. Many people come to Jesus every single day just because an "ordinary" believer chose to step out of their comfort zone and say to the person in the fast-food line in front of them, "Excuse me, but I just want to tell you that Jesus loves you and has a plan for your life." And the angels rejoice!

I have been blessed now over the years to travel the world and share Jesus with many cultures and people groups. One last story comes to mind as I close out this chapter. I was asked to preach once in a remote village in India. Right before I shared, I thought to myself how I had absolutely nothing in common with these precious people who have never heard the Gospel before. "Christianese" is not relevant in this setting. Through a translator I simply shared a Gospel message of love, power, and resurrection. As I was sharing, my eyes were fixated on two elderly women with very weathered faces. All of a sudden, as I was preaching, I saw tears stream down the faces of these two women and they gave their lives to the Jesus I was preaching about. That image is burned within me.

You see, our responsibility is to open our mouth and share and it is God's responsibility to change lives. And if God can use me, He can certainly use you! That again is why I wrote this book. To encourage you and teach you that anyone can share with others about Jesus. Anyone can bring the Kingdom of Heaven to anyone, anywhere. Whether you are a police officer, college student, stay-at-home mom, construction worker, landscaper, gas station clerk, CEO, nurse, lawyer, farmer, and the like, this book will help give you the courage and burden to reach out to those who God places in your path.

In our own journey of life, we will each meet thousands of people throughout a lifetime. Each one of those people is deeply loved by God. And you are His hands and feet on this earth to bring the Kingdom of Heaven to the world around you. This is *not* about being an evangelist. Not at all. Rather, it's about being a follower of Jesus. And those who follow Jesus will do what Jesus does—bring the Kingdom of Heaven to a hurting world.

> Life is either a daring adventure, or nothing.
> —HELEN KELLER

Chapter 4

LIVING IN LOVE

"I didn't know that love is not about what we do, but who we are, convincing others of our love for them...and about Who loves us."
—JACK FROST, *Experiencing Father's Embrace*

A FEW YEARS AGO I HAD A LIFE-CHANGING ENCOUNTER WITH the Lord. In the middle of the night I found myself standing in a very large house in Heaven. Like Paul said in Second Corinthians 12:3, whether in the body or out of the body I didn't know, but I knew that I was in Heaven. The atmosphere of Heaven was filled with such extreme joy, love, and glory. I will never forget those sweet and overwhelming sensations that I felt. Every so often when I am worshiping at our house church, Antioch Charlotte, or at my own house, I briefly feel that same sensation—the atmosphere of Heaven. As I turned a corner in the house, all of a sudden I stood face to face with Jesus and He said that He wanted to show me something.

We stood together in a large room in the house and our eyes locked in on a large pile of gold, precious jewels, crowns, and the like off to our left. As our eyes slowly scanned the room from left to right, I saw equally beautiful, large piles of treasures. Then on the far right side of the room there was a much smaller pile, perhaps only a quarter the size of the rest of the piles of treasure. That's when Jesus spoke to me, lovingly but firmly, that I was looking at my "love reward" in Heaven for how I loved on earth. I couldn't believe how much smaller my pile was than the rest of them. And that's when He told me that He wanted me to work on my love reward.

Ever since that encounter, I have been on a quest to love people the way Jesus does. And love is the most essential fruit of the Spirit when it comes to reaching people for Jesus.

Beloved, the central theme of the Gospel from beginning to end is love. Love is the greatest of all of God's commands—loving God and loving others. And if we love well, we will do all things well.

People are afraid to love, I mean really love, because love is vulnerable. Love is intimate. Love is sacrificial. Love carries risk.

I heard a quote the other day that said we should "Love people until they ask you why." And that's just it. In this day and age we live in, people are suspicious and even taken off guard when we love them without even really knowing them. But the way to someone's heart is through love.

The Gospel is love. Love is why the Father sent Jesus to earth. Love is why Jesus died and rose from the dead. Love is why He is coming back again. To know God is to know love (see 1 John 4:8).

One of the greatest keys to walking in love toward others is for each one of us to become filled with the Father's love. We cannot love each other well if we have not lived in the Father's love well.

Keep yourselves in the love of God (Jude 1:21).

An expert in the law came to Jesus once and asked:

> *"Teacher, which is the greatest commandment in the law?" Jesus said to him, "'You shall love the Lord your God with all your heart, with all your soul, and with all your mind.' This is the first and great commandment. And the second is like it: 'You shall love your neighbor as yourself.' On these two commandments hang all the Law and the Prophets"* (Matthew 22:36-40).

The most important commandment before God is to love Him with all of our heart, mind, soul, and strength. This is first and foremost in our walk with God. There is simply no way to love others well if we do not love God well. This is the greatest of all commandments. Daily we must seek to run after His heart—this is how we fall in love with Him. Oh, to encounter the Father's love! It's one of our greatest privileges as a child of God. In my book on the Father's love, I go into great detail how you can daily encounter the Father's love and embrace.

Now, the second commandment is like the first as Jesus said in Matthew 22. He also made it abundantly clear in John 13:34-35:

> *A new commandment I give to you, that you love one another; as I have loved you, that you also love one another. By this all will know that you are My disciples, if you have love for one another.*

This is a command from the heart of Jesus. This is not an option. He meant what He said and He said what He meant. The second most important way to love God is to love others as Jesus has loved us. Jesus proclaimed these powerful truths, knowing He was about to die on the cross before them all. To love—to really love—is to have the revelation of loving others the same way that Jesus loves you. The selfless life of Jesus is our greatest example of how we are to love others. The Father was very deliberate in making the first two commandments about love.

Listen to these words of Jesus:

> *But I say to you who hear: Love your enemies, do good to those who hate you, bless those who curse you, and pray for those who spitefully use you. To him who strikes you on the one cheek, offer the other also. And from him who takes away your cloak, do not withhold your tunic either. Give to everyone who asks of you. And from him who takes away your goods do not ask them back. And just as you want men to do to you, you also do to them likewise. But if you love those who love you, what credit is that to you? For even sinners love those who love them. And if you do good to those who do good to you, what credit is that to you? For even sinners do the same. And if you lend to those from whom you hope to receive back, what credit is that to you? For even sinners lend to sinners to receive as much back. But love your enemies, do good, and lend, hoping for nothing in return; and your reward will be great, and you will be sons of the Most High. For He is kind to the unthankful and evil. Therefore be merciful, just as your Father also is merciful* (Luke 6:27-36).

Close your eyes for a moment and think to yourself right now about the way you treat, respond, and react to those around you. I'm talking about your family, friends, coworkers, acquaintances, strangers, etc. We all need to love others better, right?

It's God who empowers us to love others and to see people through the lens that He sees them. We love people *through* the love of Christ.

sustain your ministry and will be rewarded in Heaven. But ministry that is not motivated by love will not be rewarded. Love has everything to do with everything.

We preach, teach, prophesy, and pray well. We do business well, give well, and do mission trips well. But above all else, we must love well.

Let's dig just a little deeper into love. My heart and prayer is that when you are done reading this chapter, you will have a fresh understanding on how love is of the highest priority in the Kingdom as we read in First 1 Corinthians 13. This chapter is absolutely essential in bringing the Kingdom of Heaven to others. Let's look at some of the verses from First Corinthians 13 a little closer.

> *Though I speak with the tongues of men and of angels, but have not love, I have become sounding brass or a clanging cymbal* (1 Corinthians 13:1).

Paul begins this chapter by saying "Though I." He's not just addressing the church here or just you and me but also referring to himself. Paul knows that he must also live out what he is writing. Everyone without exception is called to love. Paul was saying that although you may have this great, eloquent way that you present yourself or that you can preach, teach, or share with great motivation, inspiration, and power to where people are deeply moved by what you say, without love it's just a bunch of noise coming out of you. You may even have the tongues of angels, which Paul could be referring to when he was "caught up into Paradise and heard inexpressible words, which it is not lawful for a man to utter" (2 Cor. 12:4). Even then, it's just a bunch of noise, a clanging cymbal, and sounding brass without love. Our preaching doesn't move God's heart—love does. The truth is that we need to talk less and love more!

And though I have the gift of prophecy, and understand all mysteries and all knowledge, and though I have all faith, so that I could remove mountains, but have not love, I am nothing (1 Corinthians 13:2).

We know that in First Corinthians 14:1 and 39, Paul highly values the powerful and beautiful gift of prophecy. However, someone can even have extraordinary prophetic insight (we are seeing an increase of this gift in the Body of Christ today), divine revelation, and supreme knowledge of God and His plans for mankind, but without love that person is nothing in the sight of God. Imagine that—nothing! And that same person could have all faith, so that they could remove mountains, and people consider him/her God's man or woman of faith and power, flowing in signs, wonders, and miracles, but without love— again, nothing. It means nothing to God. The world, the church, my friends may think I'm somebody, but I am nothing because I do not have love. Think of it, even the most extraordinary gifts a person can have on this earth mean nothing to God without love. No reward, no blessing, nothing without love.

And though I bestow all my goods to feed the poor, and though I give my body to be burned, but have not love, it profits me nothing (1 Corinthians 13:3).

If I would give an abundance of my food and possessions to help serve and feed the poor, without love it profited me nothing in eternity. And then, imagine this—even if I gave my body to be burned as a martyr, which is very honorable, if it was not motivated by love, it does not count for eternity.

Here's the point. Everything that Paul is describing is good and honorable, but if it is not rooted and grounded in God's love it is unprofitable—no reward in Heaven. Sure, the people on earth will give you rewards, money, applause, talk about you on social media, and so on, but not God. There is no mention of it in Heaven if it was not done out of love. Sobering.

> *Love suffers long and is kind; love does not envy; love does not parade itself, is not puffed up* (1 Corinthians 13:4).

When bringing the Kingdom of Heaven to others, people can see right away by the way we are acting if we are truly a loving person.

> *By this all will know that you are My disciples, if you have love for one another* (John 13:35).

Love is tender, patient, and long-suffering with those who are not easy to have a patient, tender, and long-suffering heart toward. Especially those who have obvious flaws or faults in their life. Remember how patient and tender God is with our own faults and shortcomings. God is love. Therefore God is patient with me and you.

Love is kind. To love is to have a gentle spirit. Love is not harsh or critical. Sadly, I meet many Christians who are simply unkind and who always seem to be critical of everyone and everything—this is not love. We need to be actively looking for ways to be kind to others. As I said previously, a moment of kindness can be worth a lifetime of hope and healing for a hurting heart.

You may say, "Ryan, that's just not my personality." I'm sorry to tell you this, but that's a cop-out. I understand that you may not be a naturally kind or patient person though you try so hard. But if you would work on your love relationship with Father God, He will do a mighty work of His love within you. Then you will begin to see how kind, patient, and loving He is of you and that will overflow to others! To love others well is to have the revelation of how much Father loves you. If you are not regularly encountering Father's love, you will not know how to receive His love or give His love away to others. Love flows from Father's heart into your heart and then it flows out to the world around you.

Love does not envy. Love does not get jealous of another person's life or ministry. Genuine love gets happy for people! Love rejoices with those who rejoice. Love enjoys what other people enjoy. Love is happy that someone you know got a new car, new home, new job, etc. To envy is to actually have feelings of disdain, discontentment, and a bad attitude toward others, which can lead to making false assumptions of why others seem to be so blessed and you are not. To envy is to wonder why others are always so happy and you always feel so miserable. To envy is to judge why others are always appreciated but it seems that you are continually overlooked. Love from above is happy for people and how they are blessed rather than envying them. Love understands that true success in life and ministry stems from an abiding relationship with Jesus.

Love does not parade itself nor is it puffed up. To love is to not brag about yourself; rather, love is modest. Love is not arrogant or egotistical. Love says, "I want to hear all about what God is doing in you." Love does not say look at me! Love says, "I want to hear all about you!" This is an absolutely essential ingredient in sharing Jesus with others. There is such love in simply listening to someone's story. Love is not condescending, belittling, or hurtful. It does not cut down others to build yourself up. This is pride, and pride is *very* displeasing to the Lord.

> *But He gives more grace. Therefore He says: "God resists the proud, but gives grace to the humble"* (James 4:6).
>
> *These six things the Lord hates, yes, seven are an abomination to Him: a proud look...* (Proverbs 6:16-17).
>
> *Does not behave rudely, does not seek its own, is not provoked, thinks no evil* (1 Corinthians 13:5).

Love does not dishonor others but has a sincere respect for people. Love is courteous. To love is to simply be nice to people. Love does not complain but rather compliments. I'm talking about the cashier, the waitress, your coworkers, your spouse, your friends, and everyone in between. When we honor people out of love, they will be drawn to Christ. People are watching us all the time to see how we will react to situations that we face from day to day. And when you react out of a heart of love, Jesus is glorified. People will say, "Now that's a Christian! They seemed to have every right to get upset in that situation and they didn't." You see how people can literally be drawn to Jesus when we are not rude?

Love promotes the good in others that they don't even see in themselves. Sometimes the greatest act of love that we can do for someone on any given day is to highlight something that you appreciate in someone else. This simple act of love breaks walls down in a person's heart to set them up to receive the Kingdom.

Again, love honors others and is not self-seeking. Love does not demand its own rights nor does it have a "me first" attitude. Love says, you first. Love is unselfish. This is a major problem in the world that we live in—selfishness. But when we read about Jesus in the Gospels, people were always pulling on Him. Do this and do that for me. However, He remained amazingly unselfish. He enjoyed giving His life away for others. The very Son of God, our wonderful Savior, the King of Kings, came to serve. Please meditate for a moment on the following verses.

> *Not so with you. Instead, whoever wants to become great among you must be your servant, and whoever wants to be first must be your slave—just as the Son of Man did not come to be served, but to serve, and to give his life as a ransom for many* (Matthew 20:26-28 NIV).

The truth is that the most happy and joyful people I know are the least selfish. We cannot love and have ungodly ulterior motives. Then it's not love. It's just a façade of love. When we love, we love with "no strings attached." We don't say, "I love you if..." or "I love you, but...." This again is selfishness, not love. Love is not self-seeking, self-serving, self-obsessed, or self-absorbed.

Love does not get easily angered, easily annoyed, is not quick to get upset or mad, is not short-tempered, grumpy, grouchy, moody, or irritable. Rather, love is kind and patient under pressure. Love is fluid rather than rigid. Love goes with the flow when met with a pressured situation. Love is calm. Love keeps out-of-control feelings, moods, and emotions under subjection to the Spirit of God. Love is peaceful. Love is not defensive. Love does not overreact. Love does not seek to return evil for evil. Rather, love looks to return good for the wrong done to it. Love blesses and does not curse.

And remember that we love others through the love of Jesus that has been poured out into our own hearts.

> *The love of God has been poured out in our hearts by the*
> *Holy Spirit who was given to us* (Romans 5:5).

Are you getting the point of this chapter? When we love, I mean really learn to love, we will be highly effective for the Lord in all that we say and do. Particularly when it comes to sharing Jesus with someone who is not born again. Is it always easy to love? No. Especially when we are hurt by others. But you can never go wrong by paying back someone with love for the wrong that they did to you. Jesus is our ultimate example.

Love keeps no record of wrongs. Why? Because God is love and He does not keep record of the wrongs that we have done as we seek forgiveness. It's love to not keep an account of the wrongs done to us. Instead, love erases and forgives those who have mistreated, hurt, and wounded us. Is this always easy to do? No, but forgiveness never fails. And again, God finds it very easy to erase and forgive every wicked, sinful, and hurtful thing we have ever done because He is the very essence and fullness of love. And the more that we walk in His love, the easier it will be to love others. Love forgives and moves on. For example, let's say that you have a next door neighbor who is unsaved who did you wrong in some way. If you hold on to that offense and choose not to forgive, walk in love, and make things right, chances are you will never reach them for Jesus.

It's so amazing to me how easily people get offended at just about anything. I am talking about Christians. When we are offended it is a sign that our love walk is not where it should be with God and one another. When we get offended, it is a sign that there is an unhealed area in our own life. Every single one of us has a multitude of opportunities on a regular basis to get offended. Guess what? Get over it and move on. It absolutely does not please the Lord to hold on to offenses. Let it go and let His love flow. Again, as Christians we are commanded to love. Jesus did not ask us to try to love if we feel like it—He commanded us to love.

> *A new command I give you: Love one another. As I have loved you, so you must love one another* (John 13:34 NIV).

Sitting on the plane the other day en route to California, I was already seated when the majority of the people still hadn't boarded. As I looked at the faces of everyone coming in, a thought came to me. What if I saw someone coming down the aisle whom I knew had done me wrong or hurt me in some way? Whether they knew they had ever done that to me or not? Would my heart well up with love for them? Forgiveness? Mercy? Joy? I imagined this scenario in my heart and the

Holy Spirit showed me a few faces my heart was not right toward. I asked Jesus to forgive me so my heart could be free. What about you?

> *Does not rejoice in iniquity, but rejoices in the truth* (1 Corinthians 13:6).

Love finds no satisfaction in the shortcomings and misfortunes of others. Love takes no pleasure in seeing our brother or sister in Christ fall into sin. Rather, love seeks to restore and bind up the broken and the wounded and those caught in the clutches of sin. This is love—this is the heart of Jesus.

We see this displayed with the woman caught in the very act of adultery (see John 8:1-11). Love does not excuse or condone the sins of others, but like a thick, beautiful blanket love covers a multitude of sins.

> *Above all, love each other deeply, because love covers over a multitude of sins* (1 Peter 4:8 NIV).

Love does not take any pleasure in repeating a negative report about someone else. Rather, love joyfully promotes the good in others—those things that God sees and not what man sees.

> *The Lord does not look at the things people look at. People look at the outward appearance, but the Lord looks at the heart* (1 Samuel 16:7 NIV).

> *Bears all things, believes all things, hopes all things, endures all things* (1 Corinthians 13:7).

Love always protects. Love is a covering for others. Love defends and holds others up. And again, love covers a multitude of sins. Love walks people through their rough seasons and hard times. Love is like when Peter began to sink and Jesus was right there to lift him up—this is love.

So He said, "Come." And when Peter had come down out
of the boat, he walked on the water to go to Jesus. But when
he saw that the wind was boisterous, he was afraid; and
beginning to sink he cried out, saying, "Lord, save me!"
And immediately Jesus stretched out His hand and caught
him (Matthew 14:29-31).

When we are under the influence of love, we believe the best about others, period. Love is not suspicious. Love trusts others. Love is not unbelieving or mistrustful. Many times I have heard people say, "I just have a hard time trusting people." That statement is founded in a hurt or a wound and does not originate from God's heart. Love trusts and believes in others and is willing to take a risk over and over with the people you meet. We guard our hearts in such a way that we do not let people walk all over us, yes, but we still walk in love by believing in people and not becoming cynical. A cynical heart hides from people and doesn't like to be around others. This is not how we love. Jesus likes to be around the very people we don't like to be around.

To love is to have hope for others—even the worst of the worst. Hope is a well that should never run dry in our hearts for others. Love never, ever gives up on people. Love does not cease believing in people. No matter how hard the heart. To keep praying for people even though there seems to be little result is hopeful love. When we are looking through the lens of love, we will pray for people not how we want them to be, but how God sees them. Love is to have a hopeful outlook on people and even life itself. Every person has a "soft spot" in their heart. It may be skin deep or deeply buried, but find it and pour in the love of God.

Love perseveres. Love tarries with people. Love spends time with people. To love is to remain loyal to people. Love stands with people through their ups and downs.

Love never fails (1 Corinthians 13:8).

Love has always been. It is here today, will be here tomorrow, and will be with us forever. Love will never fail because God never fails. Heaven's very atmosphere is permeated by God's love. It's the very air you breathe in Heaven. And we want to bring Heaven to earth. We want to bring His love into our everyday lives. From the moment we wake up in the morning we must pursue His love and a heart to love others. Throughout the day, we need to ask God how we can demonstrate love to those around us. Love is a daily choice. Love isn't always felt but it can always be released. And it's the grace of Jesus and the power of the Holy Spirit and the love of the Father that gives us the ability to love. Love is to be valued more than anything else in life. Love never fails unless we fail to use it.

Your greatest weapon in bringing the Kingdom to others is authentic love. May we ask God to enlarge our hearts to receive His love and give it away to a world desperate to be loved!

> You have no authority where you don't have love.
> —HEIDI BAKER

As you learned, loving others is absolutely essential in releasing the Kingdom of Heaven to those around you. How well are you walking in authentic love? If your love walk is poor, ask the Lord to reveal to you why you struggle with loving others. If you truly love the Lord but struggle with having an authentic love for others, I want to submit to you that there may be an unhealed area in your life. God is love and God resides in every believer; therefore, you already contain within you a deep love for those around you. But to release that love is a different story. Today ask the Holy Spirit to heal and remove every area in your life that is hindering love. You may have to forgive someone. Whatever the case may be, just remember that in Heaven we are rewarded for our love for one another.

We don't just love in word but in actions. Throughout your day today, take note of how well you are responding or reacting in love to the world around you. From your own family members to the person who is taking your order at the restaurant, how are you demonstrating love? Each one of us (whether we are willing to admit it or not) has a deep desire to be loved, admired, and appreciated. Jesus said in Luke 6:31, "Do to others as you would have them do to you" (NIV). Today, make a sincere decision that each and every person you meet, no matter the situation, you are going to love them as you would want to be loved.

Chapter 5

SALT SHAKERS
AND LANTERNS

*"We are told to let our light shine, and if it does, we won't
need to tell anybody it does. Lighthouses don't fire cannons
to call attention to the shining—they just shine."*
—D.L. MOODY

WHAT'S AMAZING IS THAT IF WE WOULD JUST REALIZE that we are truly salt and light in this world, many opportunities will open up for us to share Jesus and bring the Kingdom of Heaven. Just last night I was at a steak restaurant with a friend and we were seated where people were drinking alcohol all around us. The woman next to me had obviously been drinking as she engaged me in a conversation. I began to tell her about Jesus and she got very emotional (partly because of the alcohol, I'm sure, but nevertheless). And when she walked out, I grabbed her hand and shared a little more about His love and she held my hand tight as I believe she felt the presence of God. Friends, we are salt and light.

A very close friend of mine is a police officer here in Charlotte, North Carolina. I am privileged to ride along with him from time to time as a volunteer police chaplain while he is on duty. Whether I am spending time with him in his police car or after work hours at a restaurant, he is continually shining bright for Jesus wherever he goes. I have been with him on domestic violence calls and watched him shine bright for Jesus in the midst of all the yelling. Just the other day I was there when this same police officer got down on his knees and ministered to a homeless man who was intoxicated and reeked of urine. He shares Jesus with many people he meets on the many calls he takes as a police officer. He comes in contact with people in the worst of circumstances and inserts Jesus into a world that is mostly foreign to you and me. But this is where God has him, so this is where he shines bright for the Lord.

> *You are the salt of the earth; but if the salt loses its flavor, how shall it be seasoned? It is then good for nothing but to be thrown out and trampled underfoot by men. You are the light of the world. A city that is set on a hill cannot be hidden. Nor do they light a lamp and put it under a basket, but on a lampstand, and it gives light to all who are in the house. Let your light so shine before men, that they may see your good works and glorify your Father in heaven* (Matthew 5:13-16).

Jesus says that *you* are the salt of the earth. My life as a Christian helps bring change in a situation, just as salt changes the taste of bland food when it is added. Salt is pleasant, tasty, and preserves things from becoming decayed or rotten. To us as believers, salt signifies the life-nourishing and life-giving power of a Christian's life and influence in the world.

When Jesus told the crowd in Matthew 5 that they were salt and light, He was speaking to everyone. All who believe in Him are salt and light. I like to look at it as if God has a huge salt shaker and when He sees any area that needs the Gospel, He gives that salt shaker a few shakes and places us in "mission fields" from Africa to the inner cities of America, from rural Ireland to a multi-million-dollar business. Every location in the world needs the influence of the salt—which is you and I.

As salt, you also leave people thirsty for more of God. But you must be well seasoned yourself! Can you lose your flavor?

> *Salt is good, but if the salt loses its flavor, how will you season it? Have salt in yourselves, and have peace with one another* (Mark 9:50).

The answer is yes. There are many people who call themselves Christians who have no salt in themselves, and though their life has some purpose it's basically rendered as useless before God and others.

We must stay seasoned with salt by praying, seeking God, worshiping, reading the Word, living holy, etc. People around us can sense those whose life is seasoned with salt and those who are not.

Jesus may have pointed to the sun and then to the crowd and said to them: "You are the light of the world" (Matt. 5:14). We are the light of the world because of our glorious Savior living in us.

> *Then Jesus spoke to them again, saying, "I am the light of the world. He who follows Me shall not walk in darkness, but have the light of life"* (John 8:12).
>
> *I have come as a light into the world, that whoever believes in Me should not abide in darkness* (John 12:46).
>
> *The lights shines in the darkness, and the darkness did not comprehend it* (John 1:5).

In Acts 13:47, Paul says the Lord has commanded us to be a light to the Gentiles.

> *For you were once darkness, but now you are the light in the Lord. Walk as children of light* (Ephesians 5:8).

> *But the path of the just is like the shining sun, that shines ever brighter unto the perfect day* (Proverbs 4:18).

The closer we stay to God and the more that we abide in His love and presence, the more His light will shine bright in or lives. You are a carrier of His light, presence, warmth, and glow that people desire. How bright are you shining?

Jesus said, "A city that is set on a hill cannot be hidden" (Matt. 5:14). Having been to Israel many times, I can almost see Jesus pointing toward a city on a hill (at night in the Galilee area you can literally see the flickering of the lights of cities that are set on a hill) and essentially saying, "If you are passionate about Me and for those who do not know Me, you will be like that city for all the world to see!"

> *Nor do they light a lamp and put it under a basket, but on a lampstand, and it gives light to all who are in the house* (Matthew 5:15).

When we go camping we bring along a lantern with us. And it does not matter how dark it is outside, once that lantern is lit, the entire area around us is illuminated. It does not matter how dark the spiritual darkness is around us, we are the light of the world. In fact, the darker it becomes, the easier it is for others to notice and be attracted to the light that is within you.

Remember that when we became born again, something wonderful, magnificent, life-changing, and powerful happened in our lives, so why would we want to hide it? Why would we not want others to experience the same transformation that we have experienced? Remember what it felt like when you were away from God? Maybe you were addicted to drugs, alcohol, or perversion and Jesus came and rescued you out of that pit of darkness and brought you into His marvelous light (see 1 Pet. 2:9).

Several years ago I had one of the most intense experiences I have ever had. In the middle of the night I found myself being escorted by an angel to a particular location in Hell. We got to a certain door that literally opened into Hell itself. As the door was being opened, I was slammed to the ground with a heaviness on my chest that is very difficult to describe. Imagine this: you are laying on your back on the ground. Then somehow, someone begins to very, very slowly set a 10,000-pound weight on your chest. And as that 10,000-pound weight is on your chest, it crushes you—you can't breathe, but it doesn't kill you. All you feel is the weight crushing down on you. Friends, that's the feeling I felt in this experience. I was permitted to experience what it actually feels like to never, ever have another chance to be saved. I felt what it was like to have the complete absence of God with no hope of ever getting out of Hell for all eternity. It's overwhelming to say the least. Beloved, this is what you are saving people from. Please don't ever forget that.

You are the light of the world everywhere you go. And everywhere you go, Jesus goes with you. And because He goes with you, you cannot fail!

Recently, my son and I were paying for our groceries at a major grocery store and there were two ladies standing at the cash register talking to each other. One of them said of my son, "He looks like a nice young man." I said, "Do you know why? Because He loves Jesus with all of his heart!" I will never forget what happened next. Simultaneously they immediately and out loud gave glory to God and praised the name of

Jesus! We had church! It was wonderful. The joy of the Lord hit us all simply because they saw the Light of the world shining through my son.

Friends, put yourself out there so everyone can see the light in you. They cannot snuff the light out in you because it's Jesus. I'm reminded of those birthday candles that keep their flame even though you try to blow them out. No matter what persecution you face or what people think or say about you, they absolutely cannot take away the light that is within you. However, we can hide that light if we choose to. But no more!

Notice that Jesus said that the lampstand gives light to *all* who are in the house. All in the house can see the light, which is wonderful. But how they respond to it is a different story.

If you are shining bright for Jesus, I guarantee you that right now, people around you are noticing. Your coworkers, classmates, friends, relatives, and others are noticing that something is different about you. They "taste" the salt and see the light. I feel led of the Holy Spirit right now to tell you that there are people right now in your life who are thinking to themselves, "There is something different about her. Why does he always seem so happy? What does she have going on in her life that makes her have so much peace? Why is it that when I talk to him, I feel something tugging at my heart?" Again, right now, certain people around you are thinking these types of thoughts in their hearts. Get ready for some divine appointments!

> I have but one candle of life to burn, and I would rather burn it out in a land filled with darkness than in a land flooded with light. —JOHN KEITH FALCONER

The more time you spend in the Lord's presence, the brighter you will shine and the "saltier" you will become. I believe that to the level that we are spending time with the Lord is the level that we are attractive (from the inside out) to the world around us. We have to be careful to not allow anything in our lives that will hinder the light that is to be shining out of us. Why would somebody want what you have? Especially if we live no different than anybody else. Think about that for a moment. Part of bringing the Kingdom to others is to cause them to long for what you have. This is why we must allow the light of Jesus to flow through and around us in such a way that they cannot help but be drawn into that light of Jesus.

How are you letting your light shine at home, at work, when you are with friends, at your kids' sports events, etc.? Remember that a light does not have to ask if it can be seen. Trust me, people are attracted to the light and the salt in you just when you are near. Today, as you go about your day, remember that bringing the Kingdom and sharing Jesus is not always about saying something to someone. It's also about shining bright for the Lord in the midst of a dark and sinful world and this speaks volumes to people around you—more than you know!

Chapter 6

BRINGING THE KINGDOM

"A presence oriented people naturally yield to the atmosphere of Heaven. This helps create a reality in them that shapes the culture around them."
—BILL JOHNSON

TODAY AT OUR HOUSE CHURCH, ANTIOCH CHARLOTTE, WE opened the meeting with testimonies of how our beloved community brought the Kingdom of Heaven to their various places of influence the previous week. In our community, we are blessed to have people from all walks of life, diverse backgrounds, and occupations who are passionate about being ambassadors for the King. The stories we hear each week are incredible of how God is using each and every one of them for His glory. I believe that every child of God who comes to Antioch is a minister of the Gospel.

Did you know that if you are a Christian, *you are* a minister? And not only are you a minister, but God has a specific ministry in His heart for you to do. Whether you are a plumber, pastor, pediatrician, politician, or police officer, you are a minister of the Gospel of Jesus Christ. Whatever you are specifically called to do in this life, I can tell you that part of that calling involves the following verses:

> *Therefore, from now on, we regard no one according to the flesh. Even though we have known Christ according to the flesh, yet now we know Him thus no longer. Therefore, if anyone is in Christ, he is a new creation; old things have passed away; behold, all things have become new. Now all things are of God, who has reconciled us to Himself through Jesus Christ, and has given us the ministry of reconciliation, that is, that God was in Christ reconciling the world to Himself, not imputing their trespasses to them, and has committed to us the word of reconciliation. Now then, we are ambassadors for Christ, as though God were pleading through us: we implore you on Christ's behalf, be reconciled to God* (2 Corinthians 5:16-20).

This is one ministry that every one of us is called to—the ministry of reconciliation. We *all* who were at one time away from God are now *friends with God.* And He is calling every one of us to reconcile (reunite) people back to God. That's your ministry!

Now, how that ministry is demonstrated through your life and how it's demonstrated through mine are totally different. But you *do* have a ministry. It's to reach the world around you that no one else can. If you are a public school teacher—that's your harvest field. If you are a social worker—that's your harvest field. If you are a mechanic—again, that's your harvest field. Sure you may have responsibilities at your local church as a Sunday school teacher, usher, greeter, or pastor, but that's only one part of your life where God uses you. You have to realize that no matter how involved you are in your church, there are many other areas in your life where God wants to use you to bring healing, deliverance, salvation, reconciliation, and love. What about your neighbor, coworker, the other parents from your kids' sports team, and anyone else with whom you interact on a regular basis?

The following is a quote from the late, beloved evangelist Steve Hill. He was my friend, mentor, and hero in the faith who is now with his best friend, Jesus. He spoke this out to me one evening as he was preaching during the Brownsville Revival. I transcribed it from 1999:

> Thank God for a Bible School that has a couple hundred students going out [on the streets], don't you ever stop doing that Ryan. Don't you ever stop taking them to the streets. Don't you ever stop doing that. You know what I find? I find pastors that used to go out and talk to people about Jesus, now that can't do that anymore—they're just too busy. Pastors, I want to tell you, the greatest thing you can do is put on a t-shirt and a pair of blue jeans and walk outside that stained glass building. Go open your mouth and tell someone about Jesus! Get back down to the basics of Christianity. Let them know God loves them and has a plan for their life! —STEVE HILL

We have to realize that God's heart is to seek and save the lost, the broken, the hurting, and the dying. And we have to begin to understand that people are in your life by God's perfect, eternal design.

Does that mean that every time you interact with others you are supposed to get them to pray a prayer of salvation? No. Many are not ready to receive Jesus into their hearts at that particular moment. You can't force the Kingdom of God on someone. That can do more harm than good. I never saw Jesus in the Scriptures force Himself on anyone.

He simply brought the message of the Kingdom and accompanied that message with signs, wonders, and miracles, and He has called us to do the same. And this is how we *reconcile* people back to God.

We represent and *present* Jesus to those God places in our path each day. You are an ambassador of Christ. You are a representative of Heaven. So the question is, how well does my life represent Jesus? Let's be honest. There are many Christians today who, based on the fruit of their lives, do not represent King Jesus well. It's a version of Jesus. A version of the Gospel. A watered-down version of Christianity. Why is that? Well, there is compromise and so many do not have a deep relationship with Jesus and therefore He is not represented well. When you became born again, you also became an ambassador of the Lord. And a true ambassador of the Lord is one who is absolutely devoted to Jesus and represents His heart to those they come in contact with. And not only do they represent His heart, but all that He is. His joy, power, love, healing, peace, and the like. The closer we walk with Jesus, the better we represent Him. Again, how well does your life represent Him? Do others see, feel, and hear that there is something different about you and that you are not like all the others?

Do you realize that because Jesus is alive in you, He is passionately longing every day to reveal Himself to the person you shake hands with in a business meeting or at the café or the bus stop or at the desk next to you at school or work? I love the thought of that. Because you are at a business meeting, Jesus is at your business meeting and He wants to touch those lost businessmen and women! You are an ambassador of the Kingdom. What a privilege! My prayer is that this becomes a great reality in your life.

Do you want to know why people at work sometimes act weird around you for no apparent reason? Do you want to know why people get agitated or upset at you out of the blue? Do you want to know why demons get stirred up when you are in the room? Read the following verses:

> *Now thanks be to God who always leads us in triumph in Christ, and through us diffuses the fragrance of His knowledge in every place. For we are to God the fragrance of Christ among those who are being saved and among those who are perishing. To the one we are the aroma of death leading to death, and to the other the aroma of life leading to life. And who is sufficient for these things?* (2 Corinthians 2:14-16)

We are the fragrance of Christ. What a thought! There is a fragrance that accompanies the life of a Christian. God chooses to diffuse (or makes manifest) through us the fragrance of Jesus in every place we set our foot. And to some we give off the aroma life, and to others it is the aroma of death.

To those we are near who do not have a personal relationship with Jesus, we release an aroma that seems to be offensive, judgmental, and convicting. But to those who are children of God, we release an aroma of peace, joy, love, and the like. You can see why people who do not yet have a relationship with Jesus are so irritated just because Mr. or Mrs. "Holier Than Thou" is in the room. Friend, they're convicted and they don't even know it. The spirit realm at that moment is active around you and them. There is a battle for their life. Angels and demons, warring for souls, just because you walked in the room. Do you get what I am saying? Do you see how important your life is to the Kingdom? Do you see that by the very fact you are in the room with people, you are bringing the Kingdom, even *before* you have said a word? It's the presence and aroma of Jesus in you and with you.

So do not think it strange when people "act out" around you. It's warfare. Keep loving. Keep your peace. Keep your joy. It's not you they hate. It's Jesus.

> *If the world hates you, you know that it hated Me before it hated you* (John 15:18).

Even unsaved family members have a problem when you're around. The very fact that you are in the same room or the same house causes them to be irritated and harsh because there is an aroma in the air, and it's not comfortable for them. Don't take it personally; His glory is resting on you.

> *If you are reproached for the name of Christ, blessed are you, for the Spirit of glory and of God rests upon you. On their part He is blasphemed, but on your part He is glorified* (1 Peter 4:14).

The closer our walk is with Jesus and the more we abide with Him (see John 15), the stronger this aroma will be in our lives. And the stronger the aroma is in our lives, the more influence we will have with people in our day-to-day lives.

> *The Kingdom of God is within you* (Luke 17:21).

This is one of my favorite verses in the Bible. What a wonderful privilege to have *God* living inside us. He fills the universe yet makes His home in us. That should give you fresh revelation on the verse:

> *He who is in you is greater than he who is in the world* (1 John 4:4).

Because the Kingdom of God is within us, everywhere we go, we bring the Kingdom. Whether we are in the car, at school, baseball practice, getting coffee, shopping, at work, or any other place, because *you* are there, God is there. We are the vessels He chooses to use to bring the Kingdom to the world. My heart gets so full when I talk about bringing the Kingdom of Heaven to anyone, anywhere.

For instance, when you walk into a coffee shop, everything—and I mean everything—that every single person in that coffee shop needs to be saved, healed, made whole, and delivered is living inside you. What a thought! Healing has just entered the shop because the Healer is living inside you. Salvation has just walked into the shop because the Savior lives inside you. Freedom from every sin, sickness, and bondage has just walked into the room because the Deliverer lives inside you. And once we really begin to understand this revelation, it changes how we go about each day.

And the closer we remain to His heart, the more evident and available the Kingdom within you will manifest to those around you.

For without Me you can do nothing (John 15:5).

I can speak from much experience regarding the previous verse. The more I abide with Jesus, the greater the flow of His Spirit through me. And the opposite is true—the less I abide, the less I am leaning into His heart, there is not as strong of a flow.

Now listen carefully. I believe that there is a vast difference between being used in the gifts of the Spirit and simply being so full of Jesus that people are impacted wherever you go. Now don't get me wrong, I wholeheartedly believe in the gifts of the Spirit (we will talk more about that later). The Lord will often use me in words of wisdom, knowledge, and prophecy. And I love that. But when you are just full of Jesus, there is a divine flow and everything seems to happen so naturally. The gifts of the Spirit can come and go in our lives. They are gifts and they are given as the Holy Spirit wills (see 1 Cor. 12:11). But you don't need to wait until you are given a gift by the Holy Spirit to radically touch someone's life.

Trust me, if you spend considerable time in the presence of Jesus, live a life of self-sacrifice, and become filled with God's love—just watch how mightily Jesus will use you.

Seek the gifts. Especially that you may prophesy (see 1 Cor. 14:1). But don't wait until you are gifted or mature in your gift to step out and bring the Kingdom.

Friend, right now, if you are born again the Holy Spirit is living inside you and He wants to flow through you more than you realize. The Holy Spirit is powerful and glorious. And when the Holy Spirit is manifest in your home, at a church gathering or at a restaurant, wonderful and beautiful things happen. This is bringing the Kingdom. And the rest of this book will help you take those initial steps from discerning a divine appointment to simply opening up your mouth and telling someone that Jesus loves them.

In this life you have a Partner. You have a Friend. You have a Mentor. That is the Holy Spirit. He will lead and guide you every single day to show you where and when and to whom to bring the Kingdom. There is no striving, stress, anxiety, or fear when the Holy Spirit is involved. Usually, there is a specific person the Holy Spirit wants you to share with or pray for. You do your part and God will do His part.

Again, bringing the Kingdom is simply walking into your business meeting, school cafeteria, living room, or the high school football game. You are there—He is inside you—the Kingdom is now there.

Now that you got this far in the book, no more waiting to bring the Kingdom. You don't have to wait until you have no financial pressures. You don't have to wait until you meet someone to marry. You don't have to wait until you have a better car. You don't have to wait for an invitation. You don't have to wait until your kids are grown. You don't have to wait until you get a "better" job. You don't have to wait until you have more friends. You don't have to wait for a phone call. You don't have to wait to be recognized. You don't have to wait for a confirmation. You don't have to wait for a dream or a vision. You don't have to wait to be called on. You don't have to wait until you are older. You don't have to wait for someone to give you a prophetic word. You don't have to wait for a pat on the back. You don't have to wait until you "feel it." You don't have to wait until you have more schooling. And you certainly don't have to wait until you're perfect.

You don't have to wait any longer to begin doing exactly what God has called you to do, right now, in this season. Not later—now. You are anointed, gifted, and deeply loved and adored by God. And He has great confidence in you to fulfill His call on your life. The time is short, friends. No more waiting, wondering, and wandering about.

Whatever you need to deal with, repent of, grow up in, cast out, be set free from, or healed of—get to it!

No more waiting. Bring the Kingdom.

> Joyful intimacy with God is the great power source of the Kingdom of God. —MIKE BICKLE

M ake a point wherever you go today to remind yourself that the Kingdom of Heaven is within you. Pray in the Spirit everywhere you go. Pray to release the Kingdom in the various places that you go throughout the day. In fact, let's say you go grab a coffee today. Right before you enter the store, pray:

> *Father, it is Your will that Your Kingdom come on earth as it is in Heaven. These people in this cafe need You. They need what's inside me. I pray that You release Your Kingdom through me as I walk in. Stir up the gifts within me. Highlight someone to me with whom I may share Your heart. Release Your presence, Your love, and Your power. In Jesus' name, Amen.*

Again, everywhere you go, the Kingdom of Heaven goes with you. The Kingdom goes with you on your way to work, at your job, at the store, while you are doing the laundry, at your business luncheon (the Lord just told me that someone will remember to bring the Kingdom to their business luncheon and lives will be touched!), at school, while you're hiking, and even while you are resting. All you have to do is yield to the Holy Spirit in whatever setting you find yourself today. Contact me and let me know how you brought the Kingdom today! Reviveus247@gmail.com.

have met and shared Jesus with too many people to not be convinced that every single person—no matter what they look like, act like, or what level of social status they have—is on a search for what they may or may not ever know in this life—Jesus.

> *He has made everything beautiful in its time. Also He has put eternity in their hearts* (Ecclesiastes 3:11).

What a powerful verse. I believe that every heart has eternity stamped on it, from those on death row to those who work in the White House. And that is our open door to share the Good News and bring the Kingdom of Heaven.

Just as God wrote the Ten Commandments with His finger on the stone tablets and gave them to Moses (see Exod. 31:18), God wrote *eternity* on our hearts. And eternity is the final destination for us all. No one is exempt. All of us will soon stand before God and give an account for our lives (see Rom. 14:12; 2 Cor. 5:10).

There is a place in a person's heart that only Jesus can fill. Remember what it was like before you met Jesus? You tried to fill your life with what the world had to offer. And it always led to disappointment and unfulfillment. This is why people get deeper and deeper into sin. They are trying to satisfy and quench a hunger and thirst that only Jesus can provide. And no more can the things of this world satisfy the void within a person than a tiny piece of bread can satisfy all the hungry of Africa. As Christians, we are to bring the Bread of Life and the Living Water to satisfy the longing of the people of the world (see John 6:35; 7:37-39).

The story of the Samaritan woman in John 4:4-42 is an incredible example of someone who had come to a place in her life where nothing else satisfied and she was longing for something more. I feel that this

story is a great blueprint for bringing the Kingdom of Heaven to someone. Let's pick up the story in verse 4:

> *But He needed to go through Samaria. So He came to a
> city of Samaria which is called Sychar, near the plot of
> ground that Jacob gave to his son Joseph. Now Jacob's well
> was there. Jesus therefore, being wearied from His journey,
> sat thus by the well. It was about the sixth hour.*
>
> *A woman of Samaria came to draw water. Jesus said to
> her, "Give Me a drink." For His disciples had gone away
> into the city to buy food.*
>
> *Then the woman of Samaria said to Him, "How is it
> that You, being a Jew, ask a drink from me, a Samaritan
> woman?" For Jews have no dealings with Samaritans.*
>
> *Jesus answered and said to her, "If you knew the gift of
> God, and who it is who says to you, 'Give Me a drink,'
> you would have asked Him, and He would have given you
> living water."*
>
> *The woman said to Him, "Sir, You have nothing to draw
> with, and the well is deep. Where then do You get that
> living water? Are You greater than our father Jacob, who
> gave us the well, and drank from it himself, as well as his
> sons and his livestock?"*
>
> *Jesus answered and said to her, "Whoever drinks of this
> water will thirst again, but whoever drinks of the water
> that I shall give him will never thirst. But the water that
> I shall give him will become in him a fountain of water
> springing up into everlasting life."*
>
> *The woman said to Him, "Sir, give me this water, that I
> may not thirst, nor come here to draw."*

Jesus said to her, "Go, call your husband, and come here."

The woman answered and said, "I have no husband."

Jesus said to her, "You have well said, 'I have no husband,' for you have had five husbands, and the one whom you now have is not your husband; in that you spoke truly."

The woman said to Him, "Sir, I perceive that You are a prophet. Our fathers worshiped on this mountain, and you Jews say that in Jerusalem is the place where one ought to worship."

Jesus said to her, "Woman, believe Me, the hour is coming when you will neither on this mountain, nor in Jerusalem, worship the Father. You worship what you do not know; we know what we worship, for salvation is of the Jews. But the hour is coming, and now is, when the true worshipers will worship the Father in spirit and truth; for the Father is seeking such to worship Him. God is Spirit, and those who worship Him must worship in spirit and truth."

The woman said to Him, "I know that Messiah is coming" (who is called Christ). "When He comes, He will tell us all things."

Jesus said to her, "I who speak to you am He."

And at this point His disciples came, and they marveled that He talked with a woman; yet no one said, "What do You seek?" or, "Why are You talking with her?"

The woman then left her waterpot, went her way into the city, and said to the men, "Come, see a Man who told me all things that I ever did. Could this be the Christ?" Then they went out of the city and came to Him.

In the meantime His disciples urged Him, saying, "Rabbi, eat."

But He said to them, "I have food to eat of which you do not know."

Therefore the disciples said to one another, "Has anyone brought Him anything to eat?"

Jesus said to them, "My food is to do the will of Him who sent Me, and to finish His work. Do you not say, 'There are still four months and then comes the harvest'? Behold, I say to you, lift up your eyes and look at the fields, for they are already white for harvest! And he who reaps receives wages, and gathers fruit for eternal life, that both he who sows and he who reaps may rejoice together. For in this the saying is true: 'One sows and another reaps.' I sent you to reap that for which you have not labored; others have labored, and you have entered into their labors."

And many of the Samaritans of that city believed in Him because of the word of the woman who testified, "He told me all that I ever did." So when the Samaritans had come to Him, they urged Him to stay with them; and He stayed there two days. And many more believed because of His own word.

Then they said to the woman, "Now we believe, not because of what you said, for we ourselves have heard Him and we know that this is indeed the Christ, the Savior of the world."

What was Samaria?

Who were the Samaritans? A people of mixed Jewish and Gentile ancestry who claimed descent from Jacob and worshiped the God of Israel, but felt that Mount Gerizim rather than Jerusalem was the holy site for worship. They engaged the Jews in bitter rivalry, often leading to political hostilities in Jesus' day, sometimes requiring Roman intervention.

In John 4:1-42, Jesus crosses strict cultural boundaries separating races (in the general sense of culturally distinct peoples), genders and moral status, pointing to the new and ultimate unity in the Spirit. That this Samaritan woman comes to the well alone rather than in the company of other women probably indicates that the rest of the women of Sychar did not like her, in this case because of her sexual activities. Although Jewish teachers warned against talking much with women in general, they would have especially avoided Samaritan women, who, they declared, were unclean from birth. Other ancient accounts show that even asking water of a woman could be interpreted as flirting with her—especially if she had come alone due to a reputation for looseness.

Jesus breaks all the rules of Jewish piety here. In addition, both Isaac (Gen. 24:17) and Jacob (Gen. 29:10) met their wives at wells; such precedent created the sort of potential ambiguity at this well that religious people wished to avoid altogether *(IVP Bible Background Commentary,* CRAIG S. KEENER).

As Craig Keener pointed out, Jesus' heart for the woman and the people of Sychar (pronounced soo-khar) was greater than the customs, traditions, and cultural boundaries of men. Jesus wants all men and woman everywhere to be saved!

This is good, and pleases God our Savior, who wants all people to be saved and to come to a knowledge of the truth (1 Timothy 2:3-4 NIV).

Jesus *needed* to go through Samaria. Why? Because He had a "divine appointment" to be at that well in Samaria with that woman. Jesus had many such divine appointments while He walked the earth. A divine appointment is a circumstance or event that takes place in our lives that was set up by God to bring about His plan and desire in a certain situation. Another way to say it is:

Your kingdom come. Your will be done on earth as it is in Heaven (Matthew 6:10).

And we should pray this Scripture every day to see an increase of divine appointments in our own lives.

Jesus knew that there was a divine appointment awaiting Him in the city. And if your heart is open to them, divine appointments will come your way for the rest of your life.

As I am writing this book, just in the last week I have had multiple divine appointments. From ministering to a 16-year-old runaway, to a man blaring wild music next to me in his SUV (I simply rolled down my window, got his attention, and said that Jesus loved him and has a plan for his life among other things and his heart was visibly touched), to a salesman coming to my door, to praying for a woman who needed a healing in a grocery store—just in the last week. And believe me, if I can do it, anyone can.

I think that we make these divine appointments harder than we realize. We have to learn to discern these God appointments by remaining open to the leading of the Spirit wherever we go throughout the day. Sometimes it's a subtle "nudge" from the Holy Spirit to speak life to someone. Sometimes, you have a word of knowledge for another. At other times, a great compassion and love wells up in your heart and you just have to do or say something. Sometimes a divine appointment is very obvious. Like the woman I saw the other day in the grocery store walking around in such pain with a knee brace. I felt that nudge from the Holy Spirit to pray for her. Why? She was hurting. She needed hope and healing and Jesus is the Healer and the Hope Giver. She was visibly touched when I prayed for her. Was she completely healed at that moment? Maybe. I told her to believe that she was healed from that moment on. You see, it's my job to pray and God's job to heal. I did my part by yielding to the divine appointment and I know God will do His part.

Don't make it so hard when it's so obvious. Step out of your comfort zone for Jesus. It's never really that convenient to the flesh. But we are not moved by what we feel but by the Kingdom within us. The sooner we understand this and walk it out, the better.

Sometimes it seems as if the angels of the Lord are putting people right in my path because they know I will bring the Kingdom of Heaven to them. Like when the girl standing in line next to me getting coffee started to cry. She was having difficulty breathing and she was scared. I asked her if I could pray for her and she said yes (the Holy Spirit told me she was a Christian). After I prayed, she said she was much better. I didn't have to go look for her to help her. She was standing right next to me! And then again just the other day, I was waiting to get some food to go at a Greek restaurant and there were two benches there. The one I was sitting on and another bench across the aisle. A woman who appeared to be in her late 50s or so came in for her order and sat right next me. Why didn't she take the other bench? Because God had a plan. And we talked about Jesus, eternity, and the love of God. She wants to come to our church. Divine appointments will seek you out if you are open to the flow of the Spirit.

Does this mean that I should pray for everyone I see or who sits next to me? No. Jesus didn't even do that. But my point is that you don't need a *divine invitation* for a *divine appointment*. Here's the most wonderful key to having divine appointments. Simply do what Jesus did:

> *The Son can do nothing by Himself; He can do only what*
> *he sees his Father doing, because whatever the Father does*
> *the Son also does* (John 5:19 NIV).
>
> *For I always do those things that please Him* (John 8:29).

Again, it's bringing the will of Heaven to earth. What do you see the Father doing? What do we hear the Father saying? We know this by the Holy Spirit. And the more intimate we are with the Holy Spirit, the easier it will be to discern the will of the Father because the Holy Spirit is praying the will of the Father through us:

> *Likewise the Spirit also helps in our weaknesses. For we*
> *do not know what we should pray for as we ought, but the*
> *Spirit Himself makes intercession for us with groanings*
> *which cannot be uttered* (Romans 8:26).

Knowing this, praying in the Holy Spirit continually will bring you a steady stream of divine appointments throughout your life. I have learned that the more I pray in the Spirit, it causes *my* spirit to come into alignment with the will of Heaven and then I become more focused on the Father's agenda than on my own agenda.

> *And pray in the Spirit on all occasions* (Ephesians 6:18 NIV).

I want to make it clear to you that when I go throughout my day, I am not stressed out, anxious, or worried that I may not be discerning a divine appointment. We never read about Jesus being in a hurry or running to get to another place or He would be late. If I had to strive and force a situation, it's probably not the Father's will at that moment. However, if I am led by the Spirit, praying in the Spirit, and keeping my heart open, divine appointments will come very naturally. Many times they are either very obvious or a subtle nudge from the Holy Spirit.

Have I missed divine appointments? Yes. No question about it. But you can't beat yourself up over that. Keep moving forward in God. More appointments will come.

And remember, it's not about talking to everyone. It's about talking to that one (or sometimes a group) at that moment as we read Jesus did with the Samaritan woman. Jesus was always willing to go to that *one*. Some of the greatest stories that we read in the Gospels were of that one person encounter. I think of Nicodemus, Nathaniel, Zacchaeus, Bartimaeus, Peter, Mary Magdalene, the woman caught in adultery, just to name a few.

In our story, Jesus was wearied from His journey. This trip to Samaria was around 35 miles and He was tired. Jesus, although tired from his journey, knew that this woman coming to the well was about to be changed forever.

Many times when are going about our day, we don't necessarily "feel" like talking to anyone. Or am I just the only one? We are tired, busy, have things to do, places to go, people to see. Hurry, hurry, hurry. And in the meantime we are missing out on what is going on around us.

As we read in the story, Jesus was weary but He was also watchful. He was not led by what His flesh wanted to do but what His Father *needed* Him to do. Jesus is a wonderful example of self-sacrifice. He always has time to sit and talk with you. That's just who He is and I love that about Him.

Just think about this. You are simply going about your busy day and you find yourself standing in line somewhere. And all of a sudden you feel a nudge from the Holy Spirit as if He is highlighting the person in front of you. At first you brush it off, but little did you know that God has orchestrated the events of both your day and their day for this supernatural moment. You are busy, tired (like Jesus was in the story), and just want to get out of the store, but you keep feeling that nudge. This is a training moment for you from the Lord as well as an opportunity to plant a seed of His love in a person's heart. This is where we have to make that split-second decision and choose to be led by the Spirit. You never know what that person in front of you is going through. This is *their* moment—not yours. Now go for it! You will never regret obeying the Holy Spirit.

You are never too tired to share Jesus with someone when the Holy Spirit is prompting you. You obviously can't minister to everyone. There are not enough hours in the day nor is God asking you to do that. But we must make sure that we are bringing the Kingdom to those He is highlighting to us in the moment.

As you read earlier, love goes that extra mile. Jesus was weary *in* His work, not weary *of* His work. He came to give Himself for the world.

If you get weary of those things in life that Jesus has asked you to do for Him (whatever that may be), that's a good sign that you are probably doing it in your own strength and not through the strength and power of Holy Spirit.

> *"Not by might nor by power, but by My Spirit," says the Lord of hosts* (Zechariah 4:6).

Again, like Jesus, though we may get weary *in* the work we are doing for the Lord, we do not get weary *of* the work we are doing for Him.

Ministry is not misery. It's wonderful and fulfilling when (even in the tough times) you know you are in the center of God's will. You will get tired doing the ministry that He has called you to. True ministry is hard work. There are times of great refreshing, great joy, and great harvest. But there are also times of working very hard for the Lord. I think we can all agree that in the three and a half years that Jesus ministered on earth, He worked those disciples pretty hard. Don't be afraid to work hard for Jesus. Intimacy with Jesus sustains us in the intensity of the work. But please always remember the order of ministry:

1. Ministry to God

2. Ministry to your family

3. Ministry for God

Many have reversed this order and found themselves shipwrecked in life and ministry. When the order is right, there is a divine flow of His presence in each of those areas.

> *I must work the works of Him who sent Me while it is day;*
> *the night is coming when no one can work* (John 9:4).

Let's learn from the example of Jesus and stay close to the Father. And though we may get weary from the work we do on earth, we know that one day soon there will be a great rest and reward.

But that time is not yet...

> You are someone else's miracle! God is setting up divine appointments and it is our job to keep them.
> —MARK BATTERSON

As you pray and yield to the Holy Spirit today, you are setting yourself up for divine appointments. Before you leave the house in the morning, ask the Lord to help you be sensitive to the direction of the Holy Spirit. What you thought was a mistake by forgetting to purchase something at the store, as you go back, a divine appointment is waiting on you! I believe that God would move Heaven and earth just to set up a divine appointment with a Christian and someone who needs the Kingdom brought to them.

Please realize that a divine appointment doesn't necessarily mean that the person you struck up a conversation with at work is going to fall on their knees and give their lives to Jesus (or they might!). As powerful as that is, and we have seen that many times, a divine appointment can simply be that you bought someone their lunch because they forget their wallet. And as a result of that simple act of love, you left an eternal impact on their heart. You bought them lunch with a smile, love in your heart, and a genuineness that deeply appealed to the longing in their heart. And the fact that you said Jesus loved them tied it all together in their heart. That person will never forget what you did because it was by the Spirit and in love. Don't you just love the thought of that!

Father, bring us many divine appointments!

Chapter 8

IT'S THAT EASY

"Any method of evangelism will work if God is in it."
—LEONARD RAVENILL

J ESUS BEGAN SPEAKING TO THE SAMARITAN WOMAN WITH A simple and natural sentence, "Give me a drink." Sharing Jesus and bringing the Kingdom to someone can be as easy as saying, "Can I have a drink?" or "Do you know what time it is?" or "Beautiful day today, huh?" or "Did you watch the game last night?" Friends, it's that easy to begin to dialogue with someone.

The truth is, sharing Jesus with others should be as natural as any other conversation you would have with someone. I saw a t-shirt the other day that said: "Warning: I may start talking about Jesus at any time." I love that!

I just got back from lunch with a dear friend and before he got there, I began a conversation with the guy who waited on me. I immediately discerned that there was something different about him—something clean, if you know what I mean. I simply said, "So what's your story? What brought you to this restaurant?" To make a long story short, I found out that he owned a landscaping business, was "flipping" houses and also worked as a waiter to retire at 40. I asked if he was going to be able to do that, and with a big smile he said, "Oh yeah." I asked him what he was going to do with all that free time and he said missions work! It turns out that he loves the Lord and I gave him my email address for a future connection for missions. Did you notice how easy that was? No striving. Just an easy conversation. And guess what? You can do that too. Next time you go out to dinner, try this and watch what happens!

Have you ever received some very exciting news? I mean news that was either life changing or just absolutely amazing? Maybe you just got engaged, or you inherited some money, or you just received a major job promotion or the birth of your child. What did you want to do with that news? Keep it inside? Hide it? And when you shared the news all over social media did you contain your joy and excitement? Did you hold anything back? Did you care who knew? Didn't you want to tell everyone?

You probably know where I am heading with this. By far, and with no close second, the best news that we have ever received is that Jesus loved us enough to die for us so we could forever be with Him.

The Gospel has changed my life, my sins are forgiven, and my eternal destiny is Heaven and not hell! We have been transformed from darkness into light (see Col. 1:13). The wrath of God does not abide on us (see John 3:36). You and I have this beautiful, wonderful, powerful, life-changing, exciting, glorious gift in our possession. Why would we not share it with others?

Why do you think Christians have such a difficult time sharing their faith when it should be so natural? People will sometimes reject you. Not *might* reject you, but *will* reject you and what you have to say.

And that's okay. It's not you they are rejecting anyway but what's inside you. There are keys to moving beyond the fear that I will share in the next chapter.

We have to learn to be more relatable to people. We have more in common with others than we realize. If you talk with someone long enough, you will almost always find common ground to dialogue about. Read what Paul said about this:

> *For though I am free from all men, I have made myself a servant to all, that I might win the more; and to the Jews I became as a Jew, that I might win Jews; to those who are under the law, as under the law, that I might win those who are under the law; to those who are without law, as without law (not being without law toward God, but under law toward Christ), that I might win those who are without law; to the weak I became as weak, that I might win the weak. I have become all things to all men, that I might by all means save some. Now this I do for the gospel's sake, that I may be partaker of it with you* (1 Corinthians 9:19-23).

Paul's desire was to become all things to all men. Why? To save the lost. Period.

These verses in First Corinthians 9:19-23 by no means give us any room for compromise. If you feel that you have to compromise your convictions to reach someone for Jesus, you are doing it in your own strength and not His. You can live out these verses without compromising your walk with God. I have known people who have used these verses as an excuse for their life of compromise.

Recently, we were selling our dining room set. We advertised it and a man came to my house wearing a Chicago Cubs shirt. We instantly bonded because I have always liked the Cubs, as I grew up north of Chicago as did he. We hit if off well. We talked for some time and there was no mention of Jesus. As I taught you already, I was simply being salt, light, and genuinely interested in this man who "God brought to my house." A divine appointment perhaps? Actually, I feel that anyone who comes to my house and knocks on my door or rings the doorbell is there by divine appointment! Anyway, it eventually came up about what we did for a living. I told him that among other things, I was pastor of a local church. He liked that. You see, we already bonded before this. I had an open door into his heart because we had so much in common. He said that he wanted to invite me over to watch a Cubs game sometime with his friends. He said, "But we all drink beer, is that okay?"

What would you do? What would you say? In this real-life situation, how do I "become all things to all men"? Personally, I can tell you that as a family, we do not drink alcohol. Does that mean I don't go to his house? Of course not. Will I feel pressured to drink beer when I am there, to "fit in"? Absolutely not. And this is where a lot of people miss it. They feel like they have to talk and act like the world to reach the world. And I wholeheartedly disagree.

Jesus had such a divine attraction to Him that sinners felt very comfortable being around Him. Why? Jesus was and is the most pure-hearted, uncompromising, holiest man who ever walked the earth. But sinners were drawn to Him. He was their friend (see Matt. 11:19). I love to meditate on the fact that Jesus was and is truly a friend of sinners.

When Jesus walked the earth, He carried so much love, joy, grace, peace, and mercy that everyone (that is everyone with an open heart, unlike the jealous and religious of the day) found Him irresistible. And the more our lives become like Jesus, the more the world will be drawn to us. Drawn to Jesus, that is.

Let me just warn you right here. If you are one of those who feels like you have to look and act like the world to reach the world, here's what will happen: People will be drawn to you, yes, but when they really get to know you and find out who and what you believe, they will not desire it because you really seem no different from anybody else. Why would they want your version of Jesus? People want the real thing, my friend. People are so tired of compromising Christians who share a diluted version of Jesus. Again, if you feel that you have to compromise to reach people, you are lacking the power of God and you are not trusting in His ability to reach them.

> *Do not love the world or the things in the world. If anyone loves the world, the love of the Father is not in him. For all that is in the world—the lust of the flesh, the lust of the eyes, and the pride of life—is not of the Father but is of the world. And the world is passing away, and the lust of it; but he who does the will of God abides forever* (1 John 2:15-17).

Be real with people. They want that. Why not just choose today to stand for what you believe in? Take care of any unresolved issues within your heart that make you want to compromise. It's time for you to be on fire for Jesus!

You have every right to stand for what you believe in and stand for your convictions. Jesus did. And He has given us the Holy Spirit to help us do the same. If you are reading this and you love Jesus and are still in school, I'm telling you right here that you don't have to give in to peer pressure and the Lord says to you right now, "I'v got your back at school!" Young person, stand up for what you believe in. Remember:

> *He who is in you is greater than he who is in the world* (1 John 4:4).

I have heard many Christians through the years say that they would die for the Gospel. And that is commendable. But how about having that same passion and zeal for living for the Gospel? Beloved, you can boldly stand in the face of sin, compromise, and wickedness and say, "I do not choose the things of this world; I choose Christ!"

Where are the men, women, teenagers, and children who carry the fire, are radically in love with Jesus, and hate everything sin and love everything God? It's time to "Come out from among them and be separate, says the Lord" (2 Corinthians 6:17).

We live in a world that is full of sin and darkness, but you do not have to allow the world to live in you! It's our own choice. We rub shoulders with the world every day, but the world does not have to rub off on us. Are we supposed to do our best to avoid being around the people of the world? Certainly not. Listen to what Paul said:

> *I wrote to you in my epistle not to keep company with sexually immoral people. Yet I certainly did not mean with the sexually immoral people of this world, or with the covetous, or extortioners, or idolaters, since then you would need to go out of the world* (1 Corinthians 5:9-10).

We live in this world but we are not of this world. Our "citizenship is in heaven, from which we also eagerly wait for the Savior, the Lord Jesus Christ" (Phil. 3:20).

I would have loved to have been in the same room Jesus was in as He was spending time with those labeled as sinners. Oh, how He must have loved them. He did not reject them but welcomed them. Did He ever condone their lifestyle? Never. But those are the very ones He came for!

> *I have not come to call the righteous, but sinners to repentance* (Luke 5:32 NIV).

You are going to see and hear about the sins of this world for the rest of your life. Only in Heaven will everything be pure, holy, and wonderful. So this is why we don't avoid people in this world but are always looking for opportunities to share His love and bring the Kingdom. Many Christians seem to be more concerned with the *sins* of the world than the *souls* of the world. If we get overly focused on the sin in people's lives all around us, we will not be able to know God's heart for them.

Many people I encounter have their walls up and are not willing to let them down easily. With the help of the Holy Spirit, He will use us to help people let their guards down so we can share the heart of the Father with them.

In between writing this chapter, I had dinner with my good friend, Larry Sparks, and he was an eyewitness to what happened at dinner tonight. As we were being seated at our table, our waitress came over to greet us. She had a great big smile that I pointed out. She seemed to really appreciate that. Friends, as this chapter title says, "It's That Easy." I simply and sincerely said something nice to her and she let her guard down a little bit. I asked her if she was a Christian and she said yes and that her whole family was. But it didn't end, there as the Holy Spirit had another agenda. She mentioned that she wanted to go to college and I asked her what she wanted to study. She said writing and journalism, of all things. So Larry (who is an author and publisher) and I gave her some pointers on starting a blog, etc. I told her that this was a divine appointment. Her guard was let down a little more. Do you see how easy this is? And the Holy Spirit was not done.

When she was away for a while, the Holy Spirit prompted me that He wanted me to speak into her destiny, which I did and she was visibly moved. She continued to wait on more tables and once again the Holy Spirit prompted me. He said to ask her about her father. When she came back I asked her if I could ask her a personal question (now remember her guard was down from simply showing love to her). She said yes without hesitation. I said, "Would you mind telling me about your father?" She looked at me so strange. She said that he molested her when she was young. I said, "You don't have to tell me any more details, it's okay." I told her that God doesn't show us things just to put His finger in someone's business but to bring healing. I spoke to her of the Father' love and how He wants to take that pain and hurt out of her and replace and restore it with His great love. She received it. She cried. It was beautiful. She was very thankful that we came in.

It's that easy.

In your life you will encounter all kinds of people from various walks of life and you need to have the kind of heart that easily adapts to people. We want to feel what they feel. We want to hurt for people, laugh with people, cry with people. We want to go to their homes, go to their work, go to the ends of the earth and do everything we can that we might by all means save some. This is the heart of Jesus!

Let the following quotes sink deep within your heart.

> I care not where I go, or how I live, or what I endure so that I may save souls. When I sleep I dream of them; when I awake they are first in my thoughts...no amount of scholastic attainment, of able and profound exposition of brilliant and stirring eloquence can atone for the absence of a deep impassioned sympathetic love for human souls.
> —DAVID BRAINERD

> While women weep, as they do now, I'll fight; while children go hungry, as they do now I'll fight; while men go to prison, in and out, in and out, as they do now, I'll fight; while there is a drunkard left, while there is a poor lost girl upon the streets, while there remains one dark soul

without the light of God, I'll fight—I'll fight to the very end! —WILLIAM BOOTH

If sinners be dammed, at least let them leap to Hell over our bodies. If they will perish, let them perish with our arms about their knees. Let no one go there unwarned and unprayed for. —CHARLES SPURGEON

Friends, it's that easy.

I want to let you in on a secret. There are many, many times that I feel compelled by the Holy Spirit to bring the Kingdom of Heaven to someone. Whether it's at our house church, my own home, a restaurant, or anywhere else. However, there are also many times I don't feel an unction from the Holy Spirit in the moment to say or do something to bring the Kingdom. I love people like you do, so I just tell the waitress that she is loved by God as I continue with my order. I didn't "feel" that I should say that but it's so easy to say and now an eternal seed is planted in her heart.

The other day I was at a restaurant with some of my friends and I struck up a conversation with the waitress as I asked her about a tattoo that she had on her arm. Easy question, right? Well, that led into more conversation. Then she said these very words to me: "I don't understand the cross." Inside I was like, yes! What a great question! We had a great talk as I shared with her why Jesus had to die such a brutal death but the good news is that He did that for her and rose from the dead. The presence of the Lord was so strong. All because I asked her about her unique tattoo.

I want you to try something today. With an open heart of love and authenticity, strike up a conversation with someone. You can give them a compliment, talk about a news event, or whatever comes to mind and watch how easy it is to bring the Kingdom of Heaven to that person.

Chapter 9

LIKE A PUNCH
IN THE FACE

"It was strictly forbidden to preach to other prisoners. It was understood that whoever was caught doing this received a severe beating. A number of us decided to pay the price for the privilege of preaching, so we accepted their (the communists) terms. It was a deal; we preached and they beat us. We were happy preaching. They were happy beating us, so everyone was happy."
—RICHARD WURMBRAND

I REMEMBER IT LIKE IT WAS YESTERDAY. I WAS WALKING IN THE park on a Friday night in Pensacola, Florida. We had our usual small army of students out there with us sharing the Gospel. I then noticed a man who was yelling at a number of our students. I walked up to him and struck up a friendly conversation even though he was obviously agitated. He said that he was getting tired of all the young people talking about Jesus to everyone. We spoke for only about five minutes when I turned to him again and said, "Sir..." and that's the last thing I remember as he "sucker punched" me in the face and knocked me out! As I fell, my head hit a concrete fountain in the park and that's when I came to. By the time I realized what had happened, the man was long gone. A practicing satanist we had been witnessing to over the previous weeks actually helped me get my bearings and find a seat on the park bench. I can tell you honestly that I had no anger toward the man who hit me. It was the devil in him. Father's love washed over my heart for the man. It didn't take away the pain in my head and face that I was feeling, but I knew I took that hit for Jesus. However, it was a very, very small price to pay for the Lord, compared to all that He has done for me.

In verse nine in our story, this woman at the well reminded Jesus of the hostility and tension between the Jews and Samaritans by saying, "Jews have no dealings with Samartians" (John 4:9). There are certain times when you may find yourself in tense or even hostile environments as you bring the Kingdom to others.

Remember that *you* are the light of the world and with each step of light that you take in a spiritually dark, cold place, this disturbs and stirs up the Kingdom of darkness. Wherever you go, demons know you are there with the authority, power, love, and blood of Jesus. Again, when you go to a restaurant, spend time with your family, or simply walk down the street, the spiritual realm is fully aware of your presence. And devils get easily agitated and nervous when a man or woman of God is around them.

So here's the point. You have absolutely nothing to be afraid of when bringing the Kingdom to others. You are never, ever alone: "I will never leave you nor forsake you" (Heb. 13:5).

It does not matter to what level you are persecuted or laughed at, no one can ever take from you the great joy of salvation that is in your heart—no one! It is out of their reach. Others *may* harm you physically, but they can never take away that treasure inside you. When your heart is bursting with the love of God, it fortifies your heart in such a way that it really doesn't matter what anyone says to you. Yes, people will swear at you, reject you, and say all kinds of hurtful and wicked things to and about you as they did the same to Jesus. He understands and He is with you. So there is no need for fear. You are confident in the Lord and who you are as His son and daughter.

I find it so unbelievable that many, many people who literally sat with Jesus and listened to His teachings chose to still reject Him. Did you get that? Even Jesus, the very Son of God had people laugh at Him, say He had a demon, and mock Him (see Luke 8:53; John 8:48; Matt. 27:29). Jesus performed multitudes of miracles, signs, and wonders but because of the hardness of hearts, people still chose not to believe in Him. If people did that to Jesus, they will do it to us, so don't take it personally. That should take some pressure off of you. It was the same with the apostle Paul. With all of the great revelation and understanding that Paul had, along with his powerful personal testimony, people still rejected his message of the Gospel.

Remember how in Matthew 26:69-75 Peter was afraid of the questions of a servant girl? Peter learned the hard way about being persecuted as Jesus was being interrogated. Read what Peter had to say in First Peter 3:13-17 after the Holy Spirit radically changed him from the inside out:

> *And who is he who will harm you if you become followers of what is good? But even if you should suffer for righteousness' sake, you are blessed. "And do not be afraid of their threats, nor be troubled." But sanctify the Lord God in your hearts, and always be ready to give a defense to everyone who asks you a reason for the hope that is in you, with meekness and fear; having a good conscience, that when*

they defame you as evildoers, those who revile your good
conduct in Christ may be ashamed. For it is better, if it is
the will of God, to suffer for doing good than for doing evil.

As Peter said, "always be ready." And here's the truth of the matter: "all who desire to live godly in Christ Jesus will suffer persecution" (2 Tim. 3:12). And all means all. And all means you.

If it hasn't already happened, you will—not might—but will be persecuted. It's part of the life of being a Christian. If you have never been harassed, persecuted, made fun of, look down upon, rejected, mocked, or laughed at for being a Christian, where have you been? Everyone I know who has stood for Jesus has at one time or another faced opposition for what they believe. Again, it comes with the territory of being a Christian. Listen to these precious words of Jesus:

Blessed are those who are persecuted for righteousness' sake,
for theirs is the kingdom of heaven. Blessed are you when
they revile and persecute you, and say all kinds of evil
against you falsely for My sake. Rejoice and be exceedingly
glad, for great is your reward in heaven, for so they perse-
cuted the prophets who were before you (Matthew 5:10-12).

Jesus tells us that when (not if) we are persecuted for His great name's sake, to rejoice and be exceedingly glad. There is a reward in Heaven that awaits the persecuted on earth. You could have shared with someone about football, the economy, or the weather and nothing would have happened. But when you mention the Name that is above every name, they freak out. They react the way they do because a powerful light is shining in their dark world.

Right now, I want you to be very honest with yourself and answer these questions. Am I ashamed of the Gospel? Am I ashamed of Jesus? Am I ashamed to share with others what God has done for me? Am

I afraid of being rejected or made fun of? Most everyone who is a Christian has had to answer a question like this at some point in their lives. You are not alone. And if you did answer yes to any of these questions, the first step to overcoming is realizing that you need to make a change.

At the risk of oversimplification, one of the easiest ways to bring the Kingdom to others and to be a witness for Jesus is to bring the Kingdom to others and be a witness for Jesus. Yes, just do it. Step out. Take a risk. As I taught you in the last chapter, it's easier than you realize. I am telling you, just one divine moment where you see Heaven touch earth in someone's life, you will never be the same. It will set you free of any fear or embarrassment that you may have.

When living in Pensacola, Florida, I used to try to get a dear friend of mine to come out on the streets with the other students to share Jesus. He had such a fire within him but did not feel comfortable walking up to people to share Jesus and bring the Kingdom. We had so many students going out on the streets on a Friday night (sometimes 250 students on a Friday night!) that we set up intercessory teams who would walk around the areas where we were witnessing and just pray. I reminded my friend how he loved to pray and to at least go out with one of our prayer teams. He agreed. It didn't take but a few times of going out on the streets and praying until he was hooked. He alone saw so many lives saved and discipled while he was a student. That was almost 20 years ago and he is still on fire, still winning people to Jesus; he is doing most of his ministry now in the Middle East and that's why I cannot share his name with you.

Sometimes our greatest hindrance is just stepping out that very first time. And even if the first time you bring the Kingdom of Heaven to a situation it does not turn out the way you would have hoped, don't give up. That's exactly what the enemy wants you to do. Give up and stay silent.

Can you just imagine what would happen in our world if every Christian began to rise up and bring the Kingdom? We would totally overwhelm every area of society with the presence of God. I am believing for another Great Awakening to sweep the earth; how about you?

Listen, you have absolutely nothing to be ashamed of.

> *For I am not ashamed of the gospel of Christ, for it is the power of God to salvation for everyone who believes, for the Jew first and also for the Greek* (Romans 1:16).

Remember that Paul lived during a time when you could be killed for proclaiming the Gospel and being a follower of Jesus. And preaching the Good News could mean death to anyone who declared it. These are not just passive words in Romans 1:16 to pump us up to not be ashamed of Jesus. Paul had to take into consideration that what he was doing could mean his death. Friend, what do you have to be afraid or ashamed of?

There have been men and women of God from generations before us who *stand out* because they *stood up* in their generation. They refused to be conformed *to this world* but gave their lives *for the world* to see the Kingdom of Heaven brought to earth. Will you be one of those?

If you are a believer in Jesus, you qualify to bring the Kingdom of Heaven to the world around you. But what about my past? What about my present circumstances? What about my health? What about my finances? What about this and what about that? Friend, you are loved. And isn't God greater than all of your questions? Isn't He bigger than all of your circumstances? And isn't being washed in His blood more powerful than your past or any wrong you have done? If there's one thing I know about the enemy it's that he will do whatever it takes to keep you pushed down and overwhelmed in life so you will not be effective for the Lord. The devil realizes that he can't have your soul, so he will try to take you down and steal, kill, and destroy from your life. *However*, Jesus came to give life, and that more abundantly (see John 10:10).

I know that you feel hope rising in your heart! I have a book on my shelf here in my office called *England Before and After Wesley*, referring to John Wesley and the supernatural awakening that he brought to England. And right now, there are books being written in Heaven about you. How will you change the world around you? How will your world be different "before and after" you have been there?

No more fear. Step out today and bring the Kingdom to someone around you. I close this chapter with more powerful words from one of the most changed lives in the Word of God. This is written for you today:

> *Beloved, do not think it strange concerning the fiery trial which is to try you, as though some strange thing happened to you; but rejoice to the extent that you partake of Christ's sufferings, that when His glory is revealed, you may also be glad with exceeding joy. If you are reproached for the name of Christ, blessed are you, for the Spirit of glory and of God rests upon you. On their part He is blasphemed, but on your part He is glorified. But let none of you suffer as a murderer, a thief, an evildoer, or as a busybody in other people's matters. Yet if anyone suffers as a Christian, let him not be ashamed, but let him glorify God in this matter* (1 Peter 4:12-16).

I believe that if the apostle Peter were here today, he would look you in the eye and say, "Friend, you have absolutely nothing to be ashamed of. And whatever you do, always be ready to tell people about the great hope that is inside you."

And then I can see Peter walking away and then turning back around and saying with great intensity in his eyes: "Oh, and Jesus is coming back very soon. Stay ready and don't give up."

> Therefore, I bind these lies and slanderous accusations to my person as an ornament; it belongs to my Christian profession to be vilified, slandered, reproached and reviled, and since all this is nothing but that, as God and my conscience testify, I rejoice in being reproached for Christ's sake. —JOHN BUNYAN

Part of the life of a Christian is the fact that you will be made fun of, persecuted, and rejected because of what you believe. To the world, what you believe and stand for sounds out of touch with the 21st century and just plain nonsense.

The more time we spend with Jesus and yielding to the Holy Spirit, He gives us the strength, courage, and power to overcome any level of persecution that we face.

> *But you shall receive power when the Holy Spirit has come upon you; and you shall be witnesses to Me in Jerusalem, and in all Judea and Samaria, and to the end of the earth (Acts 1:8).*

It's the Holy Spirit within us that gives us the power to be a bold and strong witness for the Lord at sports events, missions trips, the grocery store, and everywhere else! This is why we need to stay continually filled with the Holy Spirt by praying in the Spirit as much as possible.

> *But you, beloved, building yourselves up on your most holy faith, praying in the Holy Spirit (Jude 1:20).*

Ask the Lord today to forgive you for having fear or being ashamed of the Gospel. He knows you love Him. He knows that His sons and daughters are persecuted, but He is walking with you every step of the way. Be bold and unashamed today to bring the Kingdom of Heaven!

Chapter 10

PEOPLE WANT
ANSWERS

"Every Christian is either a missionary or an imposter."
—CHARLES SPURGEON

I MEET PEOPLE ALL THE TIME WHEN SHARING THE GOSPEL WHO want answers to their lifelong questions. These questions range from, "What happened to the dinosaurs?" to "If God is so good, then why did my father die in a car accident after winning the father of the year award in my city?" I will never forget that particular question when the daughter asked me with tears in her eyes. My own heart is heavy right now as I think about her asking me that question almost 20 years ago. People want answers.

It is no easy task to look someone in the eyes and talk about a loving Father in Heaven when all they have known is pain and heartache. If God is so great, why didn't He stop this or that from happening in my life? The truth is, God is good and God is great. He is and will always be everything we read about Him in the Word of God. He is "merciful and gracious, slow to anger, and abounding in mercy" (Ps. 103:8).

If you have lived on this earth long enough, you probably have experienced heartache in one way or another. For instance, I lost my father to cancer when I was only 12 years old. That wasn't fair. You talk about questions—I had plenty for God. There is just nothing you could have said to me that would have healed my broken heart. I didn't want your answers—I wanted my dad. And I meet this same scenario over and over again when I share Jesus with others. People want to know, "Where is this God you are bragging about?" in the midst of all the pain and turmoil in the world. At times, even Christians struggle with some of these same questions about God and His love, goodness, and mercy.

As just a reminder, this book is written for you to bring the Kingdom of Heaven to anyone, anywhere. I'm not only referring to the lost of the world but to your own spouse, kids, church members, and the like. We are to bring the Kingdom of Heaven to *all* that the Lord is directing us to.

The woman in our story had questions:

> Then the woman of Samaria said to Him, "How is it that You, being a Jew, ask a drink from me, a Samaritan woman?" For Jews have no dealings with Samaritans (John 4:9).

What was the woman trying to do here? She was trying to turn the conversation into a political debate and deter Jesus from what He wanted to do in her life. She had questions and she wanted answers. Does Jesus immediately answer her question? No. He met her question with great wisdom and love and said to her:

If you knew the gift of God, and who it is who says to you, "Give Me a drink," you would have asked Him, and He would have given you living water (John 4:10).

Does God have the answer for every question that you come in contact with? Yes, of course. But in the wisdom of God, I believe that some things are not revealed to us on this side of eternity. Therefore, there is no reason to try to answer someone's difficult life question apart from revelation from the Spirit of God. And even then, you have to use great wisdom if you should even say anything to the person. They may or may not even receive the truth from God's heart. That's one of the reasons why I believe the Lord reserves certain answers until we get to Heaven.

God has never told me all of the details of "why" my father died, even though he loved the Lord. I do know in part but not fully. But one thing that I do know for sure is that besides seeing my father in Heaven again one day, God is and will always be a Healer. He is "the same yesterday, today, and forever" (Heb. 13:8).

I have found a peace and love in Father God that is stronger than death. And because God has captured my heart and filled me with the Father's love, it has not only healed my heart but has also filled in all of the empty places from the loss of my father over these many years. I can boldly say to you today that though I have been through many painful circumstances in my life (as I am sure you have), my love and heart for God has strengthened and not weakened. Beloved, He is a wonderful Counselor, Friend, and Healer.

I share all this with you to remind you that *no one* deserves a superficial, opinionated answer to their deep lifelong questions. Empathize with people. "Rejoice with those who rejoice, and weep with those who weep" (Rom. 12:15).

When it is appropriate, remind people that sin entered the world and has tried to overtake mankind since the Garden of Eden and that we are living in a sin-saturated world every day. It is also worth telling people (again when appropriate) that God is not in Heaven programming us like robots to obey Him. We all have free choice. And some make horrible choices like those who get behind the wheel of car when intoxicated. God is not in the business of forcing people do what He wants. That's not love. That's control, manipulation, and fear. These are some of the main points I have made with people whose hearts are open to hear. And I usually only bring up those points when the question is more general than specific to their own life. Most of the time if I don't have an answer for someone and the Holy Spirit has not said anything to me, I simply say, "I am so sorry" or "I'm sorry I don't know the answer to that" or "I'm sorry that happened to you or that you had to go through that." And whatever you do, let the love and compassion of Jesus flow through you and you will know how to respond in the moment.

You don't have to act like you are their spiritual superhero sweeping in and carrying them off with all of their answers to the great mysteries of life. There are some things that you will not be able to answer and that's okay. Let God handle that.

What we need to do is what Jesus did and turn the question into the most important thing in the moment—the heart of the person you are speaking with. Be sensitive to their heart. Listen to the cry of their soul. Pray for ears to hear and eyes to see. I find that when I am able to look beyond their difficult questions and into their heart, they usually remain open to what God has for them in the moment. Of course, it doesn't change the fact that they just asked you a difficult question—but again, you are going to a place with them that is even deeper than their deepest questions and that is the condition of their soul. That's what Jesus has a burning desire for—the soul of the person you are speaking with.

And don't ever forget that the Holy Spirit is working on them as you are sharing. You may not be noticing any tangible results, but something is happening on the inside of them in those precious few moments. The power, love, and comfort of the Holy Spirit is far greater in these moments than anything we can do for the person. We do our part and the Holy Spirit does His part.

I love to use the Word of God when I share with people as it "always produces fruit" (Isa. 55:11 NLT). Sometimes I will quote the Word verbatim and other times I will share the Word in language that they will understand. Knowing the Word of God and "hiding it in your heart" (see Ps. 119:11) is one of the greatest tools that you possess. The Word of God is your sword (see Eph. 6:17)—not to cut people with but to allow it to pierce their souls and discern the thoughts of their hearts.

> *For the word of God is living and powerful, and sharper than any two-edged sword, piercing even to the division of soul and spirit, and of joints and marrow, and is a discerner of the thoughts and intents of the heart* (Hebrews 4:12).

Friends, the Bible is a powerful weapon in your hands. And the more of the Word you know, the sharper your sword in defeating the enemy. The Bible is not an outdated, irrelevant old book. It is filled with power, love, and the presence of God.

I did an interview on the streets not too long ago where I asked a number of people what they thought about current hot-button issues in the world such as abortion, homosexuality, government, same-sex marriage, etc. I heard so many wild answers from many different people. Most every person I spoke with had a very liberal outlook on current events. Then I asked these same people if they thought the Bible was relevant for today. To my complete surprise, almost every person said yes! It stunned me. The most liberal of thinkers we came across still felt that the Bible had real validity for today. Obviously their liberal opinions and what the Bible says are at opposite ends of the spectrum, but it was fascinating nonetheless.

Unfortunately, many Christians have moved away from using the Word in their conversations with people for fear of sounding old-fashioned or out of touch with the 21st century. And this could not be any further from the truth because the Word of God finds its way into the hardest of hearts. It's a two-edged sword that does not miss a thing! The Word of God leaves nothing hidden in a person's life, but like a mirror it reveals the heart of a person.

I remember hearing a great story told by Don Wilkerson who is the founder of the Global Teen Challenge. Many years ago, Don was sharing Jesus with people and met a man in the park. Don was carrying his Bible and the man noticed that the paper the Bible was written on would be good to smoke marijuana with. The man asked Don if he could have the Bible to smoke with. Don said, "I tell you what, if you promise to read each page that you smoke, you can have my Bible." The man promised and they parted ways. I believe it was a few years later, Don was preaching in a church in that same area where that park was. A well-dressed man came up to him and asked Don if he remembered him. Don said no. The man said he was the guy who was given the Bible to smoke with. With that, Don remembered and asked the man what happened. The man proceeded to tell Don that he smoked Matthew, he smoked Mark, he smoked Luke, and then, "John smoked me!" He read the Word of God like he promised and by the time he got to John, he became born again and was now a preacher!

Friends, the Word of God changes lives. Don't ever give up on using the Word when people are looking for answers.

What you do know—know it well. As you learn and understand more—know that well. Even if it is just a few Scriptures that you memorized. Know them well and passionately proclaim them with boldness.

People want answers. The answer is Jesus.

> We are the Bible the world is reading; we are the creeds the world is needing; we are the sermons the world is heeding.
> —BILLY GRAHAM

The Bible is easily available (especially in the U.S.) to us in written and electronic form and we never seem to be too far from accessing the Word at any given time. But how much of the Bible do you really know? The Word of God is not only Father's love letter to you, but it's your sword to come against the enemy in any given situation. But you must know the Word. Study it. Meditate on it. Memorize it. Apply it. Worship the Lord with it. Pray in tongues over it. Sing the Word. Declare the Word. Have faith in the Word of God. It is life to you. It is your victory.

Let's say that you have been bringing the Kingdom to your workplace and hearts have been open. All of a sudden, one day someone starts rumors about you and talks behind your back to discredit you. No one obviously likes to have that happen to them. And it's in those moments that you want verses like this to rise up from within you:

> For we do not wrestle against flesh and blood, but against principalities, against powers, against the rulers of the darkness of this age, against spiritual hosts of wickedness in the heavenly places (Ephesians 6:12).

Now, instead of getting mad at the person or feeling like you have to defend yourself, you realize that this is a spiritual battle going on and you will attack it in the spirit and not in the flesh. This is how we learn to use the Word of God as we bring the Kingdom to the world.

Chapter 11

IRRESISTIBLE JESUS

"There are two hundred and fifty-six names given in the Bible for the Lord Jesus Christ. And I suppose this was because He was infinitely beyond all that any one name could express."
—BILLY SUNDAY

A FEW DAYS AGO I WAS SPEAKING TO A WOMAN WHO IS HELPing to plant churches all over Russia. It was incredible to hear her speak of the wonderful strategies that the Lord has given her. But one thing she said to me stood out among everything else. She said that when she goes into a village—whether they have heard the Gospel previously or not—she says that her job is to *make Jesus irresistible* to those she is speaking to. So irresistible that they can't help but fall in love with Jesus. Don't you just love that? Irresistible Jesus.

Jesus is so completely irresistible. However, if that is true, then how come we struggle sometimes connecting with His irresistibility? The answer is found in Psalm 34:8: "Taste and see that the Lord is good."

We must willingly and joyfully choose to "taste and see" how irresistible Jesus really is. If you have never had a strawberry, you would have no idea what it tasted like unless you took a bite out of it—you must "experience" the taste of a strawberry to comprehend its wonderful flavor. It's the same with Jesus. You have to take the time out of your day to partake of the goodness, love, and joy of Jesus. And we partake through prayer, worship, praying in the Holy Spirit, meditating on Him, and through the Word of God. It's that easy! Just open up your heart and let Him fill it.

You see, if Jesus is irresistible *to you*, He will be irresistible *through you* to others. I had the privilege of ministering to a couple of drug addicts this past Saturday and this theme kept running through my heart and mind. I was internally praying, "Lord help me to make You irresistible to this couple." They listened so intently as I poured out my heart to them about Jesus. They were both visibly touched by the presence of God and kept wanting to hug my friend and me.

Right now, people are watching you. I don't mean to make you feel uncomfortable, but people you are around on a regular basis have been watching you. Why? You're different. If nothing else, they sense something is unique about you. Many times they can't figure out what it is or how to define it—but they know that they know you are different. And that's a good thing. They are drawn to you (the Light in you), as I shared earlier. That's why people will have all kinds of different reactions to you just being around them. For the most part, it's spiritual warfare around you. Always remember that and stay full of the Holy Spirit. When people get close enough to you to start asking questions about your life, give them hope!

Earlier we read in First Peter 3:15:

And always be ready to give a defense to everyone who asks you a reason for the hope that is in you, with meekness and fear.

Did you catch that? *Always. Be. Ready.*

What is the hope that is in you? It's Jesus—and everything about Him. He is *your* hope. He is *their* hope. For we "have this treasure in earthen vessels" (2 Cor. 4:7).

We are holding on to the greatest treasure in the universe. This treasure is the hope of every man, woman, and child. Give it to them. Give others this hope by sharing what is inside you. Right now, at this moment, are you ready to tell someone the reason for the hope that is in you?

You must have a fire within you if you are going to kindle a fire in someone else. If your heart is lukewarm, you are going to struggle with sharing with others what is inside you. This is why I encourage others to spend much time with Jesus and He will set you on fire and then you will carry that fire everywhere you go. You will be like Jeremiah with your "heart like a burning fire" (Jer. 20:9).

We need the baptism of fire from Jesus that John the Baptist spoke of in Matthew 3:11: "He will baptize you with the Holy Spirit and fire." Again, you receive the fire by spending time with the Man of Fire, Jesus of Nazareth. He will baptize you with a fresh baptism of His holy fire that you will carry with you wherever you go. Friends, when you are on fire for God, you know it. And others will sense it too.

We don't want to present a weak Jesus to people. He appears weak to the world sometimes because many Christians are not passionate about the hope that is within them. Which is very odd to even say. How can we not be radically passionate about the One who changed our lives, saved us, set us free, and gave us an eternal hope?

Here's how you give them hope: Give the person you are speaking with your full attention and let them feel as if they are the most important person in the world at that moment—because they are. (As I write this specific, practical portion of the teaching, I feel a strong presence of the Lord. Jesus loves to teach us the how-to's so we can do those things He is asking us to do and glorify His name.) As you are speaking to the person, whatever you do, don't become distracted by movements around you. Leave your cell phone on silent and stay focused throughout the entire conversation. The woman at the well in our story was the most important person in the world at that moment to Jesus.

You see, for the most part, people believe that the place you find God is in a church. People do not expect to find Him at a well, on the streets, in a homeless shelter, at a city park, in front of a bar, at a hockey game, in the bank, at a barbecue, at a bus stop, or in a restaurant. I *love* bringing Jesus everywhere! I love sharing the Kingdom with people at the most random times and places.

Look the person in the eye whom you are sharing with. Do not hang your head. You have nothing to be ashamed about. Jesus is with you. Leonard Ravenhill used to say: "A man that is intimate with God will never be intimidated by man."

Again, look them in the eye; feel the love and compassion of Jesus for them; and boldly, meekly, passionately, and humbly tell them about the hope that is inside you. You tell them in no uncertain terms how Jesus has changed your life. Sharing your testimony is one of the most important things you can share with someone. A testimony is believable, authentic, and organic. Rarely will someone try to dispute your testimony. And even if they did, that makes no difference to you. Because you know whom you have believed and have been persuaded that He is able to keep what you have committed to Him until that Day (see 2 Tim. 1:12).

Your testimony is powerful; don't ever forget that. You *have* a testimony no matter what it is. Whether you were homeschooled all your life and grew up in a great church or you were addicted to drugs, your testimony is just as powerful as the next person's. If you are sharing your testimony of how Jesus changed your life with someone who is unsaved or whether you are bringing a Kingdom testimony to a hurting, wounded Christian—your testimony is unique, powerful, and effective.

> *Blessed be the God and Father of our Lord Jesus Christ, the Father of mercies and God of all comfort, who comforts us in all our tribulation, that we may be able to comfort those who are in any trouble, with the comfort with which we ourselves are comforted by God* (2 Corinthians 1:3-4).

> *And they overcame him by the blood of the Lamb and by the word of their testimony, and they did not love their lives to the death* (Revelation 12:11).

There are no two experiences alike when it comes to bringing the Kingdom of Heaven to the world around us. We never want to become robotic with our sharing of the Good News. People can see right through that. One night on the streets of Pensacola, Florida, I remember how busy it was in front of a particular bar. I walked up to someone to share Jesus and they stopped me and literally said, "Okay, before you say anything, here's what you're going to tell me. You are going to tell me that Jesus loves me and has a plan for my life, right?"

Honestly, her statement took me off guard. She proceeded to tell me how many students had already told her the same thing for weeks. Now, the good news is that she didn't forget it! However, we need to be sensitive to each situation that we encounter and try not to use our religious jargon to open the door to someone's heart. Just be led by the Spirit. It's easy to begin a dialogue as I said earlier. Let's be real with people and bring them hope and not religion (more on that in the next chapter). Expect and anticipate victory when you bring the Kingdom of Heaven.

In our story in John 4, Jesus goes on to say to the Samaritan woman:

> *Jesus answered and said to her, "If you knew the gift of God, and who it is who says to you, 'Give Me a drink,' you would have asked Him, and He would have given you living water"* (John 4:10).

Jesus was offering her a gift. He was offering her hope. He was extending His loving heart to her. Don't you just love that? I love how He took the time to express His love to this woman. In His response to the woman, He was very gentle and loving and in essence was saying, "If you only knew, if only you knew. All that your precious heart has been crying out for is sitting right in front of you. The answer to your broken heart and unfulfilled life is sitting at the well with you now. The One who has known you before the foundation of the world is speaking with you—if you only knew." He is extending hope to her. She has not quite grasped it yet, but her heart is being awakened.

At this moment now, Jesus is beginning to *enlighten her to save her.* And we need to do the same. Show them Jesus. Give them hope. Show them how they never have to thirst again.

We see also in verse 10 that Jesus is offering her living water. What she needed was living water from a living God. She needed the Living Water because she was dirty and needed to be cleansed. She was hurt and wounded and in need of refreshing. She was dead and needed to become alive. She was thirsty and needed an eternal drink.

> If you teach men that God is the source of their pleasure and sin is the source of their pain, they will run to God and away from sin. —JACQUELYN K. HEASLEY

Jesus is to be the central theme of everything we do in life. For it is "in Him we live and move and have our being" (Acts 17:28). Do you find in your own life that Jesus is truly irresistible? Beloved, apart from Jesus, we can do nothing (see John 15:5). It's time to draw closer to Him.

Today, I want to challenge you to get to know Jesus in a fresh new way. We become like those we hang around with. Jesus is full of passion, desire, intense love, mercy, authority, compassion, and the list goes on and on. If you spend much time with Jesus, you will begin to walk and talk like Him and see and feel like He does. This is the goal of life isn't it? To be like Him. As Paul said in Galatians 2:20:

> I have been crucified with Christ; it is no longer I who live, but Christ lives in me; and the life which I now live in the flesh I live by faith in the Son of God, who loved me and gave Himself for me.

Your testimony is a key part of bringing the Kingdom to others. It's *your* story. Leonard Ravenill once said, "*A man with an experience of God is never at the mercy of a man with an argument.*" When was the last time you shared your testimony with someone of how much Jesus has changed your life? Don't ever forget what the Lord has done for you! How He brought you out of drugs, alcohol, perversion, anger, rebellion, religion, etc. Tell someone your story today. There is power in your testimony!

Chapter 12

RELIGION IS NOT ENOUGH

"Oh God, You are my God; early will I seek You;
my soul thirsts for You; my flesh longs for You in a
dry and thirsty land where there is no water."
—PSALM 63:1

A RELIGIOUS SPIRIT TAKES THE "GOOD" OUT OF THE "GOOD News." There is a vast difference between religion and having a relationship with Father God. Here's what religion is: Religion is like trudging through the desert and seeing a mirage in the distance. It looks refreshing. It looks like water. But the closer you get, you are let down—it was only a mirage—it was just religion. Religion is like running through a maze. You turn this way and that way, only to find another dead end. Religion in and of itself makes you feel hopeless and helpless. Religion is like building a large, cold campfire. You have the logs and twigs set up just right for the perfect blaze. You set chairs around the area for everyone to enjoy. And that's it. You never light the campfire. Everything looks good and is prepared just right with all your friends, but there is no fire, no heat, no joy. Just a cold campfire. That's religion. That's a lot of our churches today. Jesus did not come to earth to start a religion but to bring us back to the Father.

You see, in our pursuit of God, religion will never satisfy. Only a deep, personal, intimate relationship with Jesus will bring the longings of a human heart to rest. From a distance, religion may look good, feel good, and sound good, but it's only a mirage of the real thing. Religion will keep getting us to pursue a mirage if we are not careful. So what do we do when our hearts are left unsatisfied and wanting because of religion?

People cannot truly know God without an intimate relationship with Him. The Father never intended for a one-sided relationship with Him. Remember reading what Adam had in the beautiful Garden of Eden? Walking and talking with his Father. They enjoyed sweet communion together until sin entered the scene.

You see, the human heart was designed to live in Eden—communion with the Father. Anything less simply does not satisfy. People on the journey of life in this "dry and thirsty land" will many times settle for religion and not relationship. There is no true joy in religion in and of itself. Religion at best is supposed to point us to a relationship with God.

However, in man's quest for significance, identity, and the knowledge that there is something "out there" bigger than themselves, they have searched and settled for everything but Jesus. What many have found is religion. There are thousands of religions in the world and nothing will ever save and satisfy but Jesus.

Friends, religion is not enough.

We talked about religion; how about relationship? It is the desire of God that all of those who live in this world find a relationship with Him. Here's what relationship with Father God is like: It's like trudging through that same desert (our life journey) and you find yourself hungry and thirsty. In the distance you see what looks like an oasis. Could it be? The closer you get, joy begins to fill your heart as you have found an oasis!

You sit under the shade of the trees and enjoy the fruit (see Song of Sol. 2:3). You taste and see that the Lord is good (see Ps. 34:8). You are refreshed. Your heart is glad and satisfied. You feel such great peace. You have completely forgotten about the difficult journey that it took to get there. You are lovesick. You feel His presence. You enjoy His fellowship. Love for Jesus grips your heart and then your heart becomes open to receive Jesus' love for you. It's where you experience sweet communion with God. Beloved, this is relationship!

What a difference between religion and relationship.

> *The woman said to Him, "Sir, You have nothing to draw with, and the well is deep. Where then do You get that living water? Are You greater than our father Jacob, who gave us the well, and drank from it himself, as well as his sons and his livestock?" (John 4:11-12)*

This woman in our story thought that the answer was to be found in Jacob's well. Most people are looking for a natural solution to a spiritual problem. Again, they try to find answers in some form of religion or in the inferior pleasures of this world.

And the answer is always Jesus.

The woman actually begins to challenge the Lord by her response. "Are you greater...?" When people challenge you, don't be put off so easily. Listen, love, and understand where they are coming from. There is no need to overreact or become defensive or offended. Remember to love.

> *Jesus answered and said to her, "Whoever drinks of this water will thirst again, but whoever drinks of the water that I shall give him will never thirst. But the water that I shall give him will become in him a fountain of water springing up into everlasting life"* (John 4:13-14).

Here we see Jesus showing her that the things of this world are only temporarily satisfying. Let's be honest. Many people enjoy the sin that they are in. Why should they give it up? It feels good. It looks good. It smells good. Why should they walk away from something that they see as being good? They will say that their sin is not hurting anyone.

But we need to share with people and help them to see that the pleasures of sin are passing. The pleasures of sin are only for a moment and then we will all have to give account to God for the life we lived on earth. It does not matter how much money you have or what things you possess or even the lifestyle you live; it will only satisfy for a season and then the end will come.

> *Come now, you who say, "Today or tomorrow we will go to such and such a city, spend a year there, buy and sell, and make a profit"; whereas you do not know what will happen tomorrow. For what is your life? It is even a vapor that appears for a little time and then vanishes away* (James 4:13-14).

I understand that people get uncomfortable when we talk like that, which in turn makes us feel uncomfortable. But our example is Jesus. He did not hold back when He taught us to let go of this world and embrace Him.

Speaking of this very thing, Jesus said in the parable of the rich man:

> *"And I will say to my soul, 'Soul, you have many goods laid up for many years; take your ease; eat, drink, and be merry.'" But God said to him, "Fool! This night your soul will be required of you"* (Luke 12:19-20).

We need to tell people they *will* thirst again and that's why they can never seem to get enough. And that their sin will lead to more sin and that is why they never feel satisfied on the inside. Because ultimately, sin does not satisfy.

When we continually feed the fierce appetite of sin, it will inevitably come back with even more force. A sinful person will always be looking for new ways to satisfy their thirsty soul. But what they do not realize is that they are drinking from dirty, nasty, polluted water.

Now in verse 14 Jesus points her again to eternal life. He is saying, "Trust Me, listen to Me, believe in Me, daughter, and your life will be forever changed!"

Jesus was not going to force her to take a drink. You can't force someone into the Kingdom. You cannot *make* someone change their heart. You can passionately persuade them, but you cannot force them.

> *On the last day, that great day of the feast, Jesus stood and cried out, saying, "If anyone thirsts, let him come to Me and drink. He who believes in Me, as the Scripture has said, out of his heart will flow rivers of living water* (John 7:37-38).

And through us, Jesus is still crying out to the lost, hurting, thirsty, and dying to come to Him and drink. But He will not force us to receive His love.

I have been guilty of this. Many years ago when I was first stepping out in sharing the Gospel, I remember literally cornering a young guy. I told Him about Jesus and forced him to pray a prayer with me.

It was wrong. My heart was right but my method was all wrong. You cannot do the Holy Spirit's work. It's your responsibility to present the Gospel and it's His responsibility to bring the conviction and conversion. When you try to force someone to pray a prayer, you can do more harm than good.

> *The woman said to Him, "Sir, give me this water, that I may not thirst, nor come here to draw"* (John 4:15).

You can begin to see her heart open little by little. Jesus was using (as He often did) something that she was very familiar with to reach her heart—a well and water. She knew what it was like to draw out water. This was beginning to make sense to her.

You need to see that this was a way that Jesus was able to connect with her. Something that she was familiar with. That's why I like to ask people lots of questions. I genuinely want to know about their life. What do you do for a living? Are you married? Where did you grow up? And so on. Again, it's not about being religious. People don't need religion. They need His love, power, and mercy. They desperately need Jesus and you are there to help them find Him. Maybe for the very first time in their life. Maybe they are backslidden. Or maybe it's someone in your church who needs a fresh touch from God.

Beloved, bring the Kingdom of Heaven to them. Awaken their hearts. If we do not speak up in the name of Jesus, someone or something else may steal their hearts away.

> I consider that the chief dangers which confront the coming century will be religion without the Holy Ghost; Christianity without Christ; forgiveness without repentance; salvation without regeneration; politics without God; and Heaven without Hell. —WILLIAM BOOTH

We want to make sure that we are introducing people to Jesus, not a religion. When you are bringing the Kingdom to others (Christians and non-Christians alike), bring them life, hope, freedom, joy, peace, power, and love—not religion.

Many of our churches today are bursting at the seams with religion and religious activity and Christians are tired of it. They are hungry and thirsty for something more—a deeper encounter with the living God. This is why new churches (especially house churches) that are emerging everywhere are passionate about hosting His presence, making disciples, and building authentic community. Sounds like the book of Acts, doesn't it?

I want to encourage you to pray about something. Will you ask the Lord if you are supposed to be inviting people over to your house for a time of fellowship and the Word in the presence of the Lord? I am not necessarily saying that you are supposed to start a church, but why not start gathering together with like-minded people to go after God? Because people are tired of religion, they are looking for gatherings that are authentic from top to bottom. Simply start gathering, have some light food, a time of worship, testimonies, a short teaching from the Word, and pray for one another as you flow in the Spirit. Religion has made it difficult to do what I just outlined. It's so easy to gather with those who are hungry and thirsty for God—and the enemy knows that. Pray about it as it may be your time!

Chapter 13

THE MYSTERIOUS HUMAN HEART

"I never have any difficulty believing in miracles. Since I experienced the miracle of a change in my own heart."

—AUGUSTINE

YOU JUST NEVER KNOW WHAT PEOPLE ARE GOING THROUGH. And nobody knows the human heart the way God does. When you meet someone in your church or on the streets for the first time, always remember that the person you just met already has a deep life history. Therefore, we never, ever want to assume that we have people "figured out" when we meet them.

Let's say that you meet someone who is 40 years old. You don't know them well but you decide to grab coffee together. As you are sipping on your cup of coffee with this person sitting across from you, let me first tell you something—you don't know them. You don't know their heart of hearts. You don't know everything they have been through. You don't know what they love and what they hate. Apart from a few nuggets of information that the Lord may give you about them—you don't know them.

Every person who has lived long enough has a deep history. Knowing this, we must be aware of how we share the Kingdom of Heaven with people and not just share the first thing that comes to our mind. We must share the Kingdom with love, authenticity, and a real desire to see them become what God's original plan and desire is for them before the foundation of the world.

> *Your eyes saw my substance, being yet unformed. And in*
> *Your book they all were written, the days fashioned for me,*
> *when as yet there were none of them* (Psalm 139:16).

That man you met today who was nasty and haughty toward you—tomorrow he may be in desperate need of help and has become tender and open to Jesus. That boss who has been rude, selfish, and hateful toward you—tomorrow he could have an encounter with God and become a totally different person.

With all this being said, each person reacts differently when they are presented with the Gospel. No two encounters are alike. When the secrets of the heart are revealed through a word of knowledge or you share a Scripture or you simply tell someone, "Jesus loves you"—everyone reacts differently.

For instance, years ago, I was with a few of my friends as we were bringing the Kingdom to an area that was known for prostitution. I remember speaking with a prostitute about how much Father loved her, wanted to forgive, heal her heart, and set her on the path of life. I felt such love in my heart for her. She looked me in the eye and started crying and said, "I see Jesus in your eyes," and then she ran away from me as fast as she could. Everyone responds to Jesus differently.

In our story of the woman at the well, we read what happens next:

> *Jesus said to her, "Go, call your husband, and come here."*
> *The woman answered and said, "I have no husband." Jesus*
> *said to her, "You have well said, 'I have no husband,' for*
> *you have had five husbands, and the one whom you now*
> *have is not your husband; in that you spoke truly"* (John
> 4:16-18).

I don't know if this woman was married and divorced five different times, but it seems like she was currently living in sin. Whatever the case may be, my heart goes out to this women every time I read this because she was obviously broken and wounded. And that's why Jesus *needed to go through Samaria.* Please don't ever forget that.

She said, "I have no husband." Jesus began to put His loving attention on her private life. This is the point in so many lives when they began to feel that conviction of the Holy Spirit. When you are bringing the Kingdom of Heaven to someone who is unsaved or backslidden and you began to shine the Light of Jesus in a heart that is dark and cold, they will start to feel an emotional response to what you are sharing.

Over the years I have seen all kinds of people react differently to conviction. And remember, if anyone feels the conviction of the Holy Spirit, that's a good thing. It means that God is working to change someone's life.

I have seen people silently but very sincerely confess their sin. Some get down on their knees. Some shake and tremble, some weep, some eyes well up with tears, some stand there and stare at you in complete silence and conviction. Some mock, some get unbelievably angry, some laugh, some joke, some are in awe of what God is doing in them at the moment, some shake your hand and say thank you, others call you names.

But no matter how someone responds to what you are saying, the good news is that the Gospel has been shared! I just love the thought of that.

> God never clothes men until He has first stripped them, nor does He quicken them by the Gospel till first they are slain by the law. When you meet with persons in whom there is no trace of conviction of sin, you may be quite sure that they have not been wrought upon by the Holy Spirit.
> —CHARLES SPURGEON

The soil of each person's heart is different. That's why some people respond immediately to the moving of the Holy Spirit and some respond only after decades of resisting. But either way I am thankful that "with God all things are possible" (Matt. 19:26). Some people respond to Jesus like Nathaniel:

> *Jesus saw Nathaniel coming toward Him, and said of him, "Behold, an Israelite indeed, in whom is no deceit!" Nathaniel said to Him, "How do You know me?" Jesus answered and said to him, "Before Philip called you, when you were under the fig tree, I saw you." Nathaniel answered and said to Him, "Rabbi, You are the Song of God! You are the King of Israel!" (John 1:47-49).*

While others need to have a power encounter like Paul:

> *As he journeyed he came near Damascus, and suddenly a light show around him from heaven. Then he fell to the ground, and heard a voice saying to him, "Saul, Saul, why are you persecuting Me?" And he said, "Who are You,*

Chapter 14

SUPERNATURAL GIFTS

"The best gift is the one that you need at that time."
—SMITH WIGGLESWORTH

RECENTLY, WHILE IN PRAYER BEFORE FILLING IN TO TEACH A session at FIRE School of Ministry, I heard the name *Phillip*. The Spirit of God told me that it was someone's middle name in the class that I was about to teach. The Holy Spirit said that He wants to "Fill-up Phillip." Now, I only knew a few of the students by their first name, let alone someone's middle name! When I got to the classroom I asked if anyone's middle name was Phillip, and sure enough he was sitting in the front row. Needless to say, he received a touch from God that night.

I'm not going to go into great detail in this book regarding the specific gifts of the Spirit, but I want to encourage you to take the time to study them so you will know when the Holy Spirit gives a gift to you (Romans 12, 1 Corinthians 12 and 14, and Ephesians 4 are just some of the chapters to study.) The gifts of the Spirit are powerful tools to reach both the saved and the unsaved alike.

As powerful as the gifts are and as much as they are to be desired (see 1 Cor. 14:1), the gifts of the Spirit must work in tandem with the fruits of the Spirit as this is the heart of God.

> *But the fruit of the Spirit is love, joy, peace, longsuffer-ing, kindness, goodness, faithfulness, gentleness, self-control* (Galatians 5:22-23).

Being used in the gifts of the Spirit is both a tremendous privi-lege and very rewarding. It is so wonderful to see someone's life deeply touched by the Word of the Lord. Recently, I prophesied over a visi-tor at our house church and she was like, "How did you know, how did you know!?" as I was seeing in the Spirit her current living situation. I was like, "I didn't know, I didn't know! But God did." She was deeply impacted. And if I can be used in the gifts, you certainly can!

Someone else recently asked me if the Lord showed me anything about her new boyfriend. I told her no. But as we continued to dialogue, it was as if I didn't hear her anymore and the Holy Spirit said one word to me—*alcohol*. I asked her about her boyfriend's drinking and the look on her face was of utter shock. Honestly, I thought I may have missed this one. However, she preceded to tell me of his alcohol problem and how he is currently in a rehab program and she had been nervous about it. So I was able to minister to her heart.

We need these gifts in our churches, at our jobs, on the streets, in the nations—everywhere. Continuing with our story, John 4:19-22 says:

> *The woman said to Him, "Sir, I perceive that You are a prophet. Our fathers worshiped on this mountain, and you Jews say that in Jerusalem is the place where one ought to worship." Jesus said to her, "Woman, believe Me, the hour*

is coming when you will neither on this mountain, nor in Jerusalem, worship the Father. You worship what you do not know; we know what we worship, for salvation is of the Jews."

This precious women was becoming challenged and changed by the prophetic flow coming from Jesus. And I believe in these days that we are living in, God is raising up men, women, and children who flow in the gifts of the Spirit to bring Jesus to our everyday lives and places of influence.

Friends, the gifts are coming back to our churches! If you are in leadership at a local congregation, I want to encourage you to take time for the gifts to flow out of the people in your church. Don't limit the Holy Spirit by just allowing the "leadership" to be used in the gifts. There are many people sitting in your church right now who flow in the gifts and you just have to give them an opportunity.

I had a vision once where I was in a house church, and in the room there were people who were worshiping and singing songs about the Holy Spirit, such as "Holy Spirit, Thou Art Welcome in This Place." And after a while, the Holy Spirit came into the room and sat on one of the seats in the house. It was an awesome sight to watch Him sitting there. All of a sudden the worship stopped and everyone stopped singing. Just then the Holy Spirit said, "You have been singing about Me. You have invited Me to come. I am here. Now what? What do you want Me to do? I am Power! I am Love! I have what you need!" And that was it. I will never forget how passionate He was about wanting to touch the people after He had been invited. Beloved, we are good at creating an atmosphere for God to move in signs, wonders, and miracles. But let's go all the way and believe for manifestations of His presence when we discern that He wants to move.

The most important moments in any church gathering, any conversation with friends, or even when you first wake up in the morning is—*what does the Holy Spirit want to say and do right now*. The time is short, my friends. Enjoy your life to the fullest, but always remember that you carry the Kingdom within you (see Luke 17:21), so you never know what could happen.

Just the other day I was invited by the police to minister to a young man who had been fighting with his mother at an apartment complex. At first he didn't want to let me in the apartment, but then he finally let his guard down. We sat down together, and to be honest with you I had nothing in common with him in the natural. He told me his young life story about how he had been in and out of homeless shelters his whole life. He never met his father, who had passed away just after he was born. In fact, this young man said these words to me: "I have never had a good day." Isn't that sad?

As you can imagine, I began to ask the Holy Spirit to show me something about his life that would begin to encourage him. I began to share with him how God saw him. I saw that God had a plan for his life in the area of creative arts and music and he lit up. By the Holy Spirit I spoke life to him and he began to change right before my eyes. It was incredible. Then I told him about Jesus. His love. His mercy. The cross and Heaven. After about 20 minutes or so, I asked him if he wanted to ask Jesus in his heart. He said yes. I asked him again and made it clear what it meant. Again, he said yes. Just then my police officer friend walked into the apartment as I began to pray. We both witnessed the greatest sight on earth. We literally saw darkness leave this young soul and Jesus come into his heart! He was so changed. His countenance became beaming with light. One of the first things that he told us was that he wanted to hug his mom when she came home (the police officer followed up later and he did just that!).

Chapter 15

ARE YOU A GOD PLEASER?

"For do I now persuade men, or God? Or do I seek to please men?
For if I still pleased men, I would not be a bondservant of Christ."
—GALATIANS 1:10

T HERE IS SUCH JOY TO BE FOUND IN KNOWING THAT YOU ARE doing those things that please God. I want to give you permission to quit trying to get everyone around you to like you or believe in what *you feel* God has called you to do. You have to quit trying to please everybody. When you lay your head on the pillow tonight after your long day, the only thing that should matter is what Jesus thought about your day. Did I please You, Jesus?

Jesus lived to please His Father.

> *I always do the things that are pleasing to Him* (John 8:29 NASB).

And He loved to do what He saw His Father doing.

> *The Son can do nothing by himself; he can do only what he sees his Father doing, because whatever the Father does the Son also does* (John 5:19 NIV).

What pleases Jesus? What is on the heart of the Father? The answer is easy:

> *"For I was hungry and you gave Me food: I was thirsty and you gave Me drink; I was a stranger and you took Me in; I was naked and you clothed Me; I was sick and you visited Me; I was in prison and you came to Me." Then the righteous will answer Him, saying, "Lord, when did we see You hungry and feed You, or thirsty and give You drink? When did we see You a stranger and take You in, or naked and clothe You? Or when did we see You sick, or in prison, and come to You?" And the King will answer and say to them, "Assuredly, I say to you, inasmuch as you did it to one of the least of these My brethren, you did it to Me"* (Matthew 25:35-40).

What a captivating portion of Scripture. This is what pleases God. Not your website. Not your 501(c)(3). Not your fancy ministry name. Not your bank account. Not your gifts. Not your speaking engagements. It's not the size of the crowd that you can gather, but it's the size of your heart that matters.

Friends, in an era where social media has gone viral, it's nauseating at times to see so many people displaying all of their spiritual accolades. I can understand why they do it to a certain level. However, we must just do the works of Jesus wherever we go and not always feel like we have to post our latest spiritual trophy on social media. If that's your motive—that's your reward. A few superficial likes on social media. Our motive must be to please God. Period. If someone wants to take a picture or a video of someone they ministered to and post it, that's great. But please don't live to minister to people for the attention of social media. There is no heavenly reward for that. Besides all this, for every one person who posts a latest ministry picture on social media, a thousand others chose to do it as unto the Lord and just leave it at that.

> *Be sure you do not do good things in front of others just to be seen by them. If you do, you have no reward from your Father in heaven* (Matthew 6:1 NLV).

Again, I understand that it's good to post mission trip pictures and ministry pictures to keep people in touch with your ministry (especially those who support you financially). That's just fine. But I am talking about motive.

I was at a very busy pizza place today and the lady who took my money said, "I am so sick." Now, I have tell you the thought went through my mind of all the stuff she was touching as she was handing me my cup.! Nevertheless, I asked her to give me her hand and I prayed for a miracle as the line built up next to me. I have no idea if she was born again or not. And then I sat down to eat. I completely forgot to check on her later to see how she was feeling. But that's not even the point. When I grabbed her hand and prayed in front of all those people, I didn't have someone take a picture. I didn't post the encounter on Facebook (I realize I am posting it here with you, but you get the point). I didn't need someone to pat me on the back and appreciate what I did.

I believe with all my heart that in the very near future, many of God's people will be ministering to so many people that it will be commonplace to see people getting prayed for and ministered to everywhere you go. That's one of the reasons I wrote this book. To prepare your heart for not only what is coming but what you can begin to do today!

Friends, just bring the Kingdom. This pleases Jesus. He is there with you and He loves it when you do that. Remember the encounter I had in Heaven with the piles of treasure? Your reward in Heaven far outweighs any reward you may receive on earth. People on earth will forget your good deeds anyway. Jesus will never forget. He loves to watch you work for His Kingdom. He absolutely loves it. He is proud of you!

Listen to what the disciples were saying of the encounter Jesus was having with this woman:

> *And at this point His disciples came, and they marveled that He talked with a woman; yet no one said, "What do You seek?" or, "Why are You talking with her?"* (John 4:27)

Jesus lived to please the Father and did not concern Himself if the disciples agreed with Him or not.

And it's the same with you. Today, you must begin to set your heart to do those things that He is telling you to do to reach the people around you. If you feel a call to reach the homeless, start today. Get a plan together. Start raising money. Serve at a shelter. If you feel a call to reach your neighbors, it's time to invite them over for dinner. If you feel called to stand on a street corner and preach and pass out flyers, just do it. You don't need a college degree or years of Bible school to begin today to bring Jesus everywhere you go. And *do not* worry what others may think. Whatever God has put in your heart to do, that's what you are supposed to be doing. I feel that someone reading this has been called to missions and the Lord has been speaking to you about that. It's time to move forward with God's plan for your life. You are a God pleaser— not a man pleaser.

John 4:27 says that the disciples "marveled" at what Jesus was doing because it went against their traditional mindset. And people will also misunderstand and criticize what you are doing. I have had to listen to critics of the call of God on my life for years. In fact, on more than one occasion someone gave me a "word from the Lord" that was completely opposite of what God was telling me to do. You don't need man's approval to bring the Kingdom. It may be a lonely road at times, and Jesus certainly understands what that feels like. Stay strong and focused.

You are already anointed to do those things that God has called you to do. The Spirit of the Lord is upon you! (Pause and read Isaiah 61 now and let your heart be stirred and awakened.)

I believe that Isaiah 61 is the anointed, passionate heart cry of God to you and me. It's like God is saying with great enthusiasm, "I have anointed you! Now, go get My children and bring them into My Kingdom. We are in this together!"

> There was a day when I died, died to self, my opinions, preferences, tastes and will, died to the world, its approval or censure, died to the approval or blame even of my brethren or friends, and since then I have studied only to show myself approved unto God. —GEORGE MUELLER

We must live our lives to please the Lord. Period. When we stand before God one day, it's not going to matter what people thought about us but only what God thought about us. It is better to live this life with a humble, loving, faithful, pure, obedient heart, hidden away and abandoned to the Father, than to try to live to please man. If you are a man pleaser, you will be miserable. If you live to please God, you will find yourself with an inner peace and incredible joy. Why? Because the Father gets so excited when you do those things that please His heart! If you are a man pleaser, you will never feel a true release from your spirit to bring the Kingdom of Heaven to others.

Below is a list of ways to become free from a man-pleasing spirit:

1. Identify when and how you have allowed a man-pleasing spirit to come in to your life. You may have to look deep within your heart for this. He is the Healer of even the deepest places within your heart.

2. Repent of any disobedience and for having a man-pleasing spirit.

3. Renew your mind with verses in the Bible that have to do with pleasing the Lord and walking in the Spirit every day.

4. Every morning when you wake up, thank the Lord for a brand-new day to do those things that please His heart everywhere you go.

5. Be ready to bring the Kingdom today!

Chapter 16

CARRIERS OF HIS PRESENCE

"I must first have the sense of God's possession of me before I can have the sense of His presence with me."
—WATCHMAN NEE

I LOVE THE FACT THAT WE HAVE THE WONDERFUL PRIVILEGE OF carrying the presence of God with us wherever we go. And the more time we spend in His presence on a personal level, the more fruit we will bear for the Kingdom. Read these verses with an open heart and with the understanding of how much we need Him:

I am the true vine, and My Father is the vinedresser. Every branch in Me that does not bear fruit He takes away; and every branch that bears fruit He prunes, that it may bear more fruit. You are already clean because of the word which I have spoken to you. Abide in Me, and I in you.

As the branch cannot bear fruit of itself, unless it abides in the vine, neither can you, unless you abide in Me. I am the vine, you are the branches. He who abides in Me, and I in him, bears much fruit; for without Me you can do nothing. If anyone does not abide in Me, he is cast out as a branch and is withered; and they gather them and throw them into the fire, and they are burned. If you abide in Me, and My words abide in you, you will ask what you desire, and it shall be done for you. By this My Father is glorified, that you bear much fruit; so you will be My disciples (John 15:1-8).

Did you catch that? Without abiding—without spending time with Jesus and inviting Him into every aspect of our lives—we can do nothing of lasting significance for the Kingdom. But through abiding and living daily close to His heart, we will experience great fruit in our lives for His glory.

The more we are filled with His heart, the greater the influence we will have on earth. We literally become carriers of His presence when we daily yield to Him. Some may make the point that because Jesus lives in us, aren't we automatically carriers of His presence? This is true. However, there is little evidence of this truth demonstrated in lives of many Christians. Why? Because we have not learned the secret of what John the Baptist proclaimed:

He must increase, but I must decrease (John 3:30).

We are the only ones standing in the way of His presence flowing in us, through us, and out of us in a greater way. Maybe our prayers should not be so much, "Lord, I want to see more miracles in my life and ministry," but rather, "Lord, whatever You have to do in my life so that there is a continual flow of Your presence through me, do that in me." That's not the easiest prayer to pray because it comes with all kinds of flesh killing and character building. I think of how strong the presence of God was radiating out of the apostle Peter as he walked by the sick:

> *And believers were increasingly added to the Lord, mul-*
> *titudes of both men and women, so that they brought the*
> *sick out into the streets and laid them on beds and couches,*
> *that at least the shadow of Peter passing by might fall on*
> *some of them (Acts 5:14-15).*

Friends, if our shadow is not yet healing the sick, there are deeper levels of His presence that we can experience. And this deeper level will inevitably touch the world around us.

This beautiful woman at the well became a carrier of the presence of Jesus. Let's finish the story:

> *The woman then left her waterpot, went her way into the*
> *city, and said to the men, "Come, see a Man who told me*
> *all things that I ever did. Could this be the Christ?" Then*
> *they went out of the city and came to Him.*
>
> *In the meantime His disciples urged Him, saying, "Rabbi,*
> *eat."*
>
> *But He said to them, "I have food to eat of which you do*
> *not know."*
>
> *Therefore the disciples said to one another, "Has anyone*
> *brought Him anything to eat?"*
>
> *Jesus said to them, "My food is to do the will of Him who*
> *sent Me, and to finish His work. Do you not say, 'There*
> *are still four months and then comes the harvest'? Behold,*
> *I say to you, lift up your eyes and look at the fields, for they*
> *are already white for harvest! And he who reaps receives*

wages, and gathers fruit for eternal life, that both he who sows and he who reaps may rejoice together. For in this the saying is true: 'One sows and another reaps.' I sent you to reap that for which you have not labored; others have labored, and you have entered into their labors."

And many of the Samaritans of that city believed in Him because of the word of the woman who testified, "He told me all that I ever did." So when the Samaritans had come to Him, they urged Him to stay with them; and He stayed there two days. And many more believed because of His own word.

Then they said to the woman, "Now we believe, not because of what you said, for we ourselves have heard Him and we know that this is indeed the Christ, the Savior of the world" (John 4:28-42).

What a beautiful ending to a beautiful story about a beautiful woman. Her life was so radically changed that she could not help but carry Jesus—carry His presence to the rest of the city. Jesus had so touched her life that it was the most natural thing for her to do—tell the world what He did for her. Don't you love that?

I have a recent story to illustrate this. Just the other day I was getting coffee and the lady behind the counter looked like she was not in a good mood. In fact, she seemed angry. The way she was moving about even made *me* feel agitated! To be honest with you, I just wanted to grab my coffee and go. But pushing past the feeling of being annoyed, I asked her how she was doing today. She told me she had a migraine (she battled frequent migraines). Well, that explains it. I asked if I could pray for her and she said yes. As I was praying, I felt the presence of God shoot right through me into her. I asked her how she was feeling and she said, "Tingly!" I told her that that was the presence of God healing her—and that's just what happened. Migraine gone. Two days later I went back to that same place and there she was again, headache-free. But this time she went and grabbed another worker and said, "That's him, that's the one I was telling you about. That's the one who prayed for me!"

You see, one life that encounters the presence of God touches so many others. That girl will never forget what happened to her. She was touched, so she touched others.

Friends, we need to spend much time in the Lord's presence if we want to see lives touched and the very atmosphere around us changed wherever we go. Personally, I am hungrier for His presence than I have ever been in my life. I just want more of Him. I want my life (and I know you do too) to reflect the One living inside me. When I get near people, I want them to sense that something is different. I want them to *feel* something different—love, joy, peace in a way that they have never felt before. And this opens the door to many divine encounters with the world around us.

Let's not settle for anything less than His presence in our lives 24/7. And again, the more time you spend living in His presence, getting to know His heart for you and the world, the greater fruit you will bear for His Kingdom.

Being a carrier of His presence is to get to know the agenda of Heaven—the Father's plans—and living from that every single day. Think about how much His presence has touched you over the years. I long for people to experience the same thing. It starts with me. It starts with you. You must become filled to overflowing. For those who "hunger and thirst for righteousness...shall be filled" (Matt. 5:6).

You must excavate everything in your life that does not please the Lord. Root it out of your life. Rid yourself of all that hinders your intimate walk with God.

Blessed are the pure in heart, for they shall see God (Matthew 5:8).

Pursue...holiness, without which no one will see the Lord (Hebrews 12:14).

Listen to what the late revivalist Gypsy Smith once said:

> Go home. Lock yourself in your room. Kneel down in the middle of the floor, and with a piece of chalk draw a circle around yourself. There, on your knees, pray fervently and brokenly that God would start a revival within that chalk circle.

I have done this. I want to encourage you to do the same. God is attracted to faith. Get hungry. Stay thirsty for Him. And never, ever, under any circumstances stop running after His heart.

Okay, today, don't talk about revival—**be revival!** You **are** the next move of God! When the Holy Spirit was poured out on the day of Pentecost, it forever changed everyone who was in the room. There were tongues of fire, the wind of the Holy Spirit, and they were drunk in the Spirit. What seemed out of the ordinary to all who were affected was **normal** for the Holy Spirit! The same Holy Spirit who was poured out in Acts 2 is living inside you! That is so amazing to me. The very Power, Presence, and Person of the Holy Spirit is inside you. And you carry Him with you wherever you go. You **are** a carrier of the presence of God.

As we are wrapping up this book, I want to passionately remind you that to the level you are yielded to the Holy Spirit, denying yourself, faithful, obedient, and walking in love and purity, is the level that you will manifest His presence in your life. His amazing, beautiful, and powerful presence is *already* inside you; that's *not* the issue. For, "the Spirit of him who raised Jesus from the dead is living in you" (Rom. 8:11 NIV). The issue is the flow *out* of you. We would save ourselves from much heartache and drama of this world if we lived with a continual flow that not only affected our own lives but those around us. If you are filled to overflowing with His presence, it will inevitably touch the world around you. But it starts with you—today. Here's where you start:

> *Therefore, since we are surrounded by such a great cloud of witnesses, let us throw off everything that hinders and the sin that so easily entangles. And let us run with perseverance the race marked out for us* (Hebrews 12:1 NIV).

There is literally a cloud of witnesses cheering you on and filled with excitement about the destiny on your life! Abraham, King David, Moses, Isaiah, John Wesley, Charles Finney, Peter, Jesus—they all believe in you and what God has called you to do.

As this Scripture in Hebrews says, what is hindering you today? What sin is entangling you? I feel that for the most part, you know what those things are. A sinful lifestyle—a continually giving in to the flesh and holding on to the pain, shame, and disappointments of your past—hinders a flow of His presence in our lives. We make things harder on ourselves by not yielding to the Holy Spirit. Many Christians are worn out and feel like giving up because of all of our earthly entanglements. But the good news is the Lord is for you. He wants you to make it to the end and not give up. He does not plan failure for your life but success. There is a race marked out for you that only you can run. The Kingdom of God is within you to accomplish *all* that you are supposed to do on this earth.

Steve Hill and I had the privilege of spending time with Bill Bright, the founder of Campus Crusade for Christ, just days before he died. Steve asked Bill to please share with us something that we could take with us before we left. Bill said, "Every day when I wake up I say, 'Jesus, these are Your hands, Your feet, Your mouth, Your eyes, and Your hands. I give them to You today for You to use them for Your glory. Not my will but Yours be done.'" I will never forget those precious moments with Bill Bright.

Today, God is asking you if you will bring the Kingdom of Heaven everywhere you go. Will you? The choice is yours, my friend. You are abundantly loved!

Chapter 17

FINAL THOUGHTS

"Preach the Gospel at all times, and when necessary use words."
—St. Francis of Assisi

I WANT TO LEAVE YOU WITH SOME FINAL MISCELLANEOUS thoughts on bringing the Kingdom of Heaven everywhere you go. Some of these are more on the practical side with a few quotes thrown in.

Don't feel pressured to feel like you always have to pray a salvation prayer with someone. Sometimes people are not ready to do that. The goal is not to get them to pray a prayer but for you to bring the Kingdom the way the Holy Spirit is showing you in the moment. However, as much as you can, ask people if they will let you pray with them about anything. I have prayed for so many people who wanted nothing to do with God, but once they give me that open door to pray, *anything* can happen!

Follow up. This is so important. As much as I am able, I leave people with my email or our church information to follow up with them. God did not call us to make converts but disciples!

> *And Jesus came and spoke to them, saying, "All authority has been given to Me in heaven and on earth. Go therefore and make disciples of all the nations, baptizing them in the name of the Father and of the Son and of the Holy Spirit, teaching them to observe all things that I have commanded you; and lo, I am with you always, even to the end of the age." Amen* (Matthew 28:18-20).

You will make mistakes when bringing the Kingdom of Heaven to people. It's part of the maturing process. But whatever you do, don't give up!

> The Great Commission is not an option to be considered; it is a command to be obeyed. —HUDSON TAYLOR

When you are bringing the Kingdom to people, you are also engaging in spiritual warfare. Stay strong and sharp in the Spirit!

> *Finally, my brethren, be strong in the Lord and in the power of His might. Put on the whole armor of God, that you may be able to stand against the wiles of the devil. For we do not wrestle against flesh and blood, but against principalities, against powers, against the rulers of the darkness of this age, against spiritual hosts of wickedness in the heavenly places. Therefore take up the whole armor*

of God, that you may be able to withstand in the evil day, and having done all, to stand. Stand therefore, having girded your waist with truth, having put on the breast-plate of righteousness, and having shod your feet with the preparation of the gospel of peace; above all, taking the shield of faith with which you will be able to quench all the fiery darts of the wicked one. And take the helmet of salvation, and the sword of the Spirit, which is the word of God (Ephesians 6:10-17).

Be sure to go out with joy and be led by peace! Sharing Jesus with others brings such glory to the Father and He loves it when you do it.

For you shall go out with joy, and be led out with peace; the mountains and the hills shall break forth into singing before you, and all the trees of the field shall clap their hands (Isaiah 55:12).

Sometimes when you are bringing the Kingdom of Heaven to a certain area (especially as a group), the police may get involved in one way or another. Always be respectful and allow the Holy Spirit to speak through you and give you wisdom. If you get an attitude with the police, it will almost always lead to more trouble. I have literally seen Christians get arrested for being belligerent and argumentative with the police. Remember, love comes first.

Always remember, you really don't know to what extent the things that you are sharing are affecting the listener. You would be surprised! Keep sharing all that you feel the Holy Spirit is giving you.

Never forget the power of prayer and intercession when bringing the Kingdom to the areas you are sharing.

Try not to interrupt the person you are sharing Jesus with.

Do not be satisfied with just leading one person to Jesus. Keep going after more souls!

It needs to be clear to people that you have a firm belief in the truths that you are sharing, otherwise they will not believe what you have to say. You do not want to be caught proclaiming to others what you do not fully believe yourself. People can tell if you have been saturated by the subject you are speaking about. If your heart is not behind what you are sharing or you do not care whether others felt or believed what you are saying, you are merely an actor performing the part. As soon as bringing the Kingdom becomes a routine, you fall into the trap of becoming a performer. Stay continually close to the heart of God to stay fresh.

Charles Spurgeon said, "If you have only a feeble appreciation of the Gospel you profess to deliver, it is impossible for those who hear your proclamation of it to be greatly influenced by it."

> Perhaps if there were more of that intense distress for souls that leads to tears, we should more frequently see the results we desire. Sometimes it may be that while we are complaining of the hardness of the hearts of those we are seeking to benefit, the hardness of our own hearts and our feeble

apprehension of the solemn reality of eternal things may be the true cause of our want of success. —Hudson Taylor

Remember that God longs to use you to rescue people from the fires of Hell. Every person you come in contact with is just one heartbeat away from Heaven or Hell.

> Give me one hundred preachers who fear nothing but sin and desire nothing but God, and I care not whether they be clergymen or laymen, they alone will shake the gates of Hell and set up the kingdom of Heaven upon Earth.
> —JOHN WESLEY

Don't be put off by those who say, "You're judging me!" You are simply bringing the Kingdom. You are not judging them. That's conviction they are feeling.

Be sincere and passionate about bringing the Kingdom to the world around you. Look at the car salesmen, actors, athletes, and so forth. They are so passionate about the things of this world. How much more should Christians be passionate for bringing the Kingdom to others?

Martin Luther tells this story:

> The devil held a great anniversary, at which his agents were convened to report the result of their several missions. "I let loose the wild beasts of the desert," said one, "on a caravan of Christians; and their bones are now bleaching on the sands." "What of it?" said the devil; "their souls are all saved."

> "I drove the east wind," said another, "against a ship freighted with Christians, and they were all drowned." "What of it?" said the devil; "their souls were all saved." "For ten years I tried to get a single Christian asleep," said a third, "and at last I succeeded, and left him so!" Then the devil shouted, and the night stars of hell sang for joy.

Another great way to bring the Kingdom is to do what many call *friendship* or *servant evangelism*. We can bring the Kingdom this way by helping and serving others so they can be drawn to God through our love, kindness, and serving. There are literally thousands of ways that you can bring the Kingdom this way. Some people are reached by what you *do* for them and not necessarily what you *say* to them. This is why our church body, Antioch Charlotte, is so strong. Because we do more than preach—we live it out with one another and those around us.

I like to encourage people to be creative in making a tract of their personal testimony. I have made my own. It's a great way to put something in someone's hand when you don't really have time to talk to them at length. Make it short and be clear without a bunch of Christian lingo in it. Put a salvation prayer at the end and maybe an email address (email is better than a phone number for safety's sake). I try to carry these with me wherever I go.

People are unreasonable, illogical and self-centered;
Love them anyway.
If you do good, people will accuse you of selfish, ulterior motives;
Do good anyway.
If you are successful, you win false friends and true enemies;
Succeed anyway.
If you find serenity and happiness, they may be jealous;
Be happy anyway.
The good you do today will be forgotten tomorrow;
Do good anyway.
Honesty and frankness make you vulnerable;
Be honest and frank anyway.
What you spent years building may be destroyed overnight;
Build anyway.
People really need help but may attack you when you help them;
Help people anyway.
Give the world the best you have and you'll get disparaged and ridiculed;
Give the world the best you've got anyway.
You see, in the final analysis, it is between you and God;
It was never between you and them anyway.
—MOTHER TERESA

Chapter 18

———————
———————
———————

YOUR TOP TEN LIST

"To be a soul winner is the happiest thing in this world."
—CHARLES SPURGEON

I WANT TO THANK YOU FOR TAKING THE TIME TO READ THIS book. My prayer in writing this book is that you will have a new passion and excitement to bring the Kingdom of Heaven to anyone, anywhere, at any time. Now, I want you to think (and pray) of ten people you currently know who you feel need the Kingdom of Heaven to come and invade their lives. Ten people who you can carry His presence to. It could be someone in your own house, church, where you work, a distant family member, someone at your kids' baseball practice, and so on.

Now in the lines provided (I gave you plenty of lines for the future), write down their names. When you are done with that, take the time every day to pray over your list and watch how the doors will begin to open for you to bring the Kingdom to those people! Write down the date that you began to pray for them and write a few notes about what

God may be saying to you about each person. Then write the testimony of what God did for them. And whatever you do, don't ever stop praying for them until your prayers are answered! Please feel free to contact me with any questions, comments, or testimonies that you may have.

YOUR TOP TEN LIST

_____

_____

_____

_____

_____

_____

_____

_____

_____

_____

_____

_____

_____

_____

_____

_____

_____

_____

ABOUT RYAN BRUSS

Revive International was founded to take the Gospel of Jesus Christ to the nations of the world. Ryan Bruss has had the privilege of traveling to many countries seeing people saved, healed, and delivered! With a passion for revival and the Father heart of God, Ryan has seen the power of God displayed in salvations, prophecy, and miracles from house churches to open-air meetings. Besides traveling to minister, Ryan, along with an amazing group of passionate believers, pastors a house church in Charlotte, North Carolina called Antioch Charlotte. Ryan and his beautiful wife Megan have been married for over 20 years and they have two wonderful teenagers, Elianna and Andrew.

If you would like Ryan to come and minister, please contact us at: reviveus247@gmail.com or you can visit our websites at: www.reviveus.org or www.antiochcharlotte.org.